Wendell Berry
and the
Given Life

R<small>AGAN</small> S<small>UTTERFIELD</small>

franciscan
media
Cincinnati, Ohio

. . . . . .

FOR MY DAUGHTERS, LILLIAN AND LUCIA,
THAT THEY MAY FIND DELIGHT IN THE GRACE OF
THE GIVEN WORLD.

. . .

Cover and book design by Mark Sullivan
Cover image © Guy Mendes

LIBRARY OF CONGRESS CATALOGING-IN-PUBLICATION DATA
Names: Sutterfield, Ragan, author.
Title: Wendell Berry and the given life / Ragan Sutterfield.
Description: Cincinnati : Franciscan Media, 2017. | Includes bibliographical references.
Identifiers: LCCN 2016057557 | ISBN 9781632531223 (hc/jkt)
Subjects: LCSH: Berry, Wendell, 1934- | Christianity—Meditations. | Conduct of life—Meditations. | Ecotheology.
Classification: LCC BX4827.B44 S88 2017 | DDC 277.3/082092—dc23
LC record available at https://lccn.loc.gov/2016057557

ISBN 978-1-63253-122-3

Published by Franciscan Media
28 W. Liberty St.
Cincinnati, OH 45202
www.FranciscanMedia.org

Printed in the United States of America.
Printed on acid-free paper.
17 18 19 20 21 5 4 3 2 1

CONTENTS

• • •

FOREWORD *by Bill McKibben* | *v*

CHAPTER ONE: GIVENNESS | *1*
Wendell Berry and the Art of Being a Creature

CHAPTER TWO: HUMILITY | *13*
Coming to Terms with Reality

CHAPTER THREE: LOVE | *24*
It All Turns on Affection

CHAPTER FOUR: ECONOMICS | *36*
Home and Care in the Kingdom of God

CHAPTER FIVE: WORK | *48*
Tilling and Keeping the Creation

CHAPTER SIX: SABBATH | *64*
Delight and the Reorientation of Desire

CHAPTER SEVEN: STABILITY | *76*
Becoming Native in an Age of Everywhere

CHAPTER EIGHT: MEMBERSHIP | *89*
Joining the Community of Creation

CHAPTER NINE: THE BODY AND THE EARTH | *101*
Reclaiming Connection in a World of Division

CHAPTER TEN: LANGUAGE | *113*
Truth and the Work of Imagination

CHAPTER ELEVEN: PEACEABLENESS | 126
Living in Harmony with the Whole of Creation

CHAPTER TWELVE: THE PROPHET | 137
Lament, Imagination, and the Renewal of Religion

AFTERWORD: A CONVERSATION WITH WENDELL BERRY | 151

SOURCES | 155

NOTES | 157

ACKNOWLEDGMENTS | 157

If one were to try to embarrass Wendell Berry, which is actually a fairly fun game, you could do worse than to start by calling him our new St. Benedict. I think if you went on to Mahatma—Great Soul—he might actually get annoyed. He is a perfectly normal man in many respects: a drier wit (often absent from his writing), a keener attention. But nothing that resembles piety in any of the ways we normally think about it.

And yet I think this book is on the entirely correct track when it imagines him as a spiritual leader of sorts. The monastery is, of course, a place of work as much as contemplation (and the lines between them often blurred); Gandhi's ashram was as devoted to spinning (in the old sense of the word) as to organizing.

It is correct to read Berry's work as a guide to the virtues, especially those usually neglected in our world: humility, for instance (if there were a literal opposite to Donald Trump on the planet, it would be Wendell Berry); or stability in time and place: or peaceableness. But there are other gurus of some of those disciplines. Berry also bears witness—relentlessly—to a value that most of our high-consumer culture has actively disparaged: community, the idea that we are more than our individual selves, the idea that indeed we really only exist in relation to those around us, both human and otherwise.

That idea of community used to go unspoken. Everyone believed in it because everyone required it. But in the second half of the twentieth century, in most of America, neighbors became optional. If you have a credit card and an Internet connection, you don't even really need to go to the grocery store anymore. And yet, the fastest growing part of our food economy for years has been the farmers market, an ancient form that Wendell Berry did more than any other living soul to revive. And the joy of the farmers market is not just the fresh produce; it's the fact, as sociologists discovered, that we have ten times more conversations per visit when we go there than when we head to the Piggly Wiggly or the Stop & Shop.

If religion is in some sense an attempt to help us understand what we were built for—why we're here—then I think that has been Berry's quest as well. Too much modern Christianity doesn't give us much of a clue: the megachurch owes more to the mall than to the catacomb. But where it fails, Berry's essays and poems and, perhaps especially, his fiction provide us with a working and workable account of what life might look and feel like properly lived. It's hard to read the Gospels and not want to come away emulating in some way the life of Jesus; it's hard to read Berry and not want to be a side-hill farmer in the southeast United States. In both cases, it's the hard and necessary work of the reader to transpose the scene into their own lives; this insightful volume helps with that task, for which I am deeply grateful.

Bill McKibben

August, 2016

CHAPTER ONE

Givenness

WENDELL BERRY AND THE ART OF BEING A CREATURE

D ust storms rage across cornfields, crops collapse from disease, the world is on the brink of mass starvation. Science has fallen from favor, seen by many as having caused the unraveling that is now plaguing the country. From the wreckage of Industrial[1] civilization, a few people rebuild combines and work to keep row-crop agriculture going a little longer—the only hope for food anyone can imagine.

This is the world of *Interstellar*, a movie whose plot leads to a secret NASA plan to save the human race by finding another planet, another place to which they can escape. Through innovation and intellect, mixed with a love that can be quantified, humanity saves itself, spinning in space stations where food is grown in a chemical medium, Earth and its soil now long ago left behind.

The movie is a fiction, but more than that it is a fantasy, a story of the hidden desires of many a human heart. It pictures the idea that humanity will save itself in the end, that we are our own masters, that we can clean up our own messes. It is a fantasy in which self-made men and self-made women create a self-made world that is controllable and predictable and so much better than the given one that failed against the rise of human ambition. *Interstellar* is the story of a human fantasy that has a long history from the tower of Babel to our current rush to modify genes—an effort to make the world rather than receive it, to create rather than be created.

Anglican theologian and former Archbishop of Canterbury Rowan Williams has described this desire to create our own world as a "deeply rooted aversion to our own creatureliness."[2] This is our original sin, the step that leads to our continued attempts to "be as gods" rather than to accept our lives as creatures formed from soil. As Williams writes, "Being creatures is learning humility, not as submission to an alien will, but as the acceptance of limit and death."[3] In our age when we strive to make our daily existence ever more responsive to our will, our desires answered by the swipe of a credit card or a command to our iPhone's Siri, living a life given rather than made is to move against the grain of the age. "Being a creature," writes Williams, "is in danger of becoming a lost art."[4]

To develop an art, we need practices and virtues; we need a community life in which such an art can be cultivated. Scottish philosopher Alisdair MacIntyre, in his classic work *After Virtue,* argues that such coherent communities are hard to find in our age. He finds an example of what our own time needs in St. Benedict, who, by organizing monasteries, created a form of community life that was able to carry civilization through the Dark Ages that followed the dissolution of the Roman Empire. "What matters at this stage," writes MacIntyre, "is the construction of local forms of community within which civility and the intellectual and moral life can be sustained through the new dark ages which are already upon us."[5] To help us create such communities, MacIntyre writes that "we are waiting...for another—doubtless very different—St. Benedict."[6]

In a very different sort of book, farmer and writer Gene Logsdon takes up the same example as MacIntyre. Logsdon, however, has an idea of what the community life we are looking for is:

> Sustainable farms are to today's headlong rush toward global destruction what the monasteries were to the Dark Ages: places to preserve human skills and crafts—until some semblance of common sense and common purpose returns to the public mind.[7]

If sustainable farms are our monasteries, our refuges for the cultivation of virtue, then we might ask: who is our St. Benedict?

Only history can answer that question, but this is a book that hopes to show that Wendell Berry presents us with the sort of coherent vision for the lived moral and spiritual life that we need now. Berry's work helps us remember our givenness and embrace our life as creatures. His insight flows from a life and practices, and so it is a vision that can be practiced and lived. What Berry writes is not about some abstract moralism. His is a coherent understanding of creatureliness that is born from soil and husbandry and home.

In all of this, Berry's vision is also deeply Christian. Though his relationship with institutional religion is often troubled (he has described himself as a "forest Christian" and a "bad-weather churchgoer"), Berry's insights are not only formed in the Christian faith, but also offer the careful reader an excellent introduction to the Christian life. He lives from the Gospels, as will become clear, and has been particularly moved by the Sermon on the Mount. His own commitments to peacemaking are born directly from Jesus's teachings—teachings that Berry has collected and published with an introductory essay as *Blessed Are the Peacemakers*.[8] How his Christianity plays out in his thought will become clear, I hope, in more detail over the course of this book.

Berry's work is, in a way, evangelistic, not only in the ideas it puts forward, but in its spiritual call. People do not read Berry, typically, and go about their business as they have before. In his work, they are given good news about how life might be in the world and many cannot help but want to go out and try it. Whether it is buying different kinds of food in the store or at farmers markets, planting a garden, or even entering the Christian faith (all responses I've witnessed), Berry's message is one that strikes a chord with a reality that is full of goodness.

Like St. Benedict, he provides a vision that many people respond to not only with their minds, but with their lives. And like Benedict, Berry would be the first to say that this vision is not his own, but one of a given goodness to which he is only pointing, even if more artfully and truthfully than most others are able to do.

• • •

Who is Wendell Berry, this possible St. Benedict for our time? I can't offer a full biography. As Berry quipped in an interview in the *New York Times Book Review*, most of his life "is beyond writing and beyond words."[9] What I can offer is a sketch of his place and his history, his influences and occupations, based on my visits to Berry's place some years ago.

Berry lives on a farm just outside of Port Royal, Kentucky. The dirt road that leads there winds past old tobacco barns, their breezy slats weathered and in disrepair. This was once tobacco country before the subsidies mostly stopped. Berry was at one time a tobacco grower, as were his father and grandfather.

His grandfather was born and died on a farm not far away, spending eighty-two years learning from the place and caring for it. Berry's father was a man who had the opportunity to leave, working for a time in Washington, DC, for a Kentucky congressman. Once he graduated, his powerful friends sought out powerful jobs for him in the city, but as Wendell Berry recounts: "My father asked himself, 'Do I want to spend my life looking out at tar roofs? Or do I want to look at bluegrass pastures?' He decided for the pastures."[10]

In returning, Berry's father set the path his son would follow. Having been elsewhere, he knew the value of the place, its culture and its economy. He became a leader in the New Deal "Tobacco Program" and its defender. In this too, he set an example for his sons. In their different ways, Wendell and his brother, John, have lived as farmers and defenders of farmers and farmland.

Lanes Landing is a working farm, reflecting care, but is also wild in its beauty. When one comes to it, there is a barn on the left, Cheviot sheep milling around and, on my visit, an old sheep dog, busy but companionable. To the left is a white farm-house up a steep hill, a drive and stairs leading to its wide front porch, which overlooks the Kentucky River valley below. There is a piano in the living room, and several pieces of original art that reflect tastes that would correct any assumptions that this farmer writer is "folksy" or "provincial."

The piano is played mostly by Tanya, Berry's wife. She has been his partner in the economy of the place and the labor of language that has flowed from it. The two met at the University of Kentucky where Wendell was studying English, completing both bachelor's and master's of arts degrees. Tanya's father was a painter, and so she grew up familiar with some aspects of artist's life that she and Berry have embodied in their own way.

There are bookshelves in the back left corner of the room. They are filled with literature, some of it from Berry's friends and colleagues. Gary Snyder has been, perhaps, Berry's closest literary friend, but he studied with and has remained close to many others. After completing his master's, Berry studied creative writing under Wallace Stegner at Stanford. It was an elite program, and Berry's colleagues would go on to be some of the most notable writers of their generation, including Ernest Gaines, Edward Abbey, Larry McMurtry, and Ken Kesey.

Beyond the house, there is a garden, and, up the hill, solar panels. Living so close to coal country, Berry is ever conscious of the destruction of the land inherent in any innocent flip of the light switch. He is not innocent, though, and it troubles him that he has to make use of a car "to be helpful to [his] neighbors." Still he works much of his land with horses as his family has done for generations.

Past the house, the road moves through timber stands and pastures. On the left, in one stand of timber, there is a room on stilts, overlooking the Kentucky River. This is Berry's writing studio, lit by natural light that streams from a gridded window that has sometimes been Berry's poetic subject, framing his "window poems."

A little farther down is another barn with an old work horse retired to a life of easy grazing wandering about outside. Inside, a boat is stored that serves as another writing studio, an open air rig from which to enjoy the river.

The land is mostly hilly with flats in the river valley. It could not hold larger animals without erosion, which is why Berry has chosen sheep as the primary produce of his farm.

Berry has never been a full-time farmer. For many years, he taught English at the University of Kentucky and, for a time, he was an editor for Rodale Press. Beyond those off farm jobs, he has managed to make a literary life and livelihood—producing a host of novels, essay collections, and volumes of poetry. But farming and its rhythms, its lessons of fidelity and care, have been at the heart of his work from the beginning. Farming is more than a job for Berry; it is not "employment," but a way.

That Berry has not been a full-time farmer should not make one imagine that his place is a "hobby farm." It is a productive landscape whose work would keep most anyone as busy as they like, but it is also not something outside of his person, a diversion from the everyday that is entailed in the idea of a hobby. It is a landscape that embodies his life, but more so it is a landscape in which his life is included in a long history of living that includes others, human and animal, geological and floral and sylvan.

• • •

Berry would describe himself as an amateur farmer, just as he would also call himself an amateur writer, though a National

Endowment for the Humanities Medal and membership in the prestigious American Academy of Arts and Letters, much less fifty books, might make one balk at such a designation. All good work, for Berry, is in some way *amateur* work—going back to the word's roots, which mean "for the love of it." Danger comes, in Berry's view, if our work is not directed by affection.

His work, then, from farming to writing is for the love of it and not only the work itself, but the larger goods that the work serves. To draw another parallel with St. Benedict, Berry sees a blurry line between work and prayer. There is a deep good in caring for one's own and one's place. And also good work has a way of forming us; it is in itself a kind of spiritual discipline.

One gets this sense from reading Berry. His concern with farming is not simply with its role in sustaining the landscape or renewing countryside communities. He sees the act of farming as getting at something deep in the human vocation—a means by which we cultivate the flourishing of creation and are in turn cultivated in our humanity through that work. One of the hallmarks of good work is this cultivation, and one of the problems with bad work is that it moves in the opposite way, degrading rather than growing. He points to the patterns of his plowed fields, noting the ways the furrows run to prevent erosion.

Berry is known, in many circles, as an advocate for small scale, sustainable agriculture—a father of the "local food movement." In other places, he is known as a literary artist—a poet and novelist. But his work is really that of the creaturely life, particularly the human form of that life. The varied forms his work has taken are in response to the infinite variability of this great subject of creation.

As a student and teacher of English literature, his work is very much in line with the tradition of the humanities. This tradition is not an abstract university department, but the accumulation of those competencies by which people have most profoundly reflected on what it means to be a human creature. Berry wants to see human life as entangled in the life of the whole creation, free from the tendency among some to see the creation as some mere terrarium-like landscape made purely for human use and entertainment. At the same time, he does not draw the kind of crass equivalence with other creatures that others tend toward, especially the kind represented in the materialist visions of neo-Darwinians such as E.O. Wilson or Richard Dawkins. Berry sees the human person as a being called toward a unique creaturely life. This is a life that is powerful and yet limited, a life of reflection and intelligence, and yet ignorance. To be human is to live in the balance of these capacities and limits, to move entirely to one side of the balance would be monstrous, or to the other side a diminishment.

What Berry calls for is humane science and humane literature, humane farming and humane art. The idea that these are divided into reified and separate categories is, in fact, a part of the problem. Part of being human is being whole, and, for Berry, the devil plays in our dichotomies and departments, our divisions and separations. In writing and in farming, his life in its place, shows the possibility of wholeness in its beauty. It invites us toward the integrity we need now.

• • •

What we need is integrity of person and creation. This impulse shows up, as we will see in more detail, throughout the whole of Berry's work. In *The Unsettling of America*, Berry's enduring major statement on the unraveling of ecological and working landscapes in America, he names the "ecological crisis as a crisis of character."

After recounting a scandal in which it was revealed that many environmental organizations had their money invested in the very organizations they were supposedly fighting against, Berry writes that, "The difficulty is that although the investments were absurd, they were *not* aberrant.... These conservation groups were behaving with a very ordinary consistency; they were only doing as organizations what many of their members were, and are, doing as individuals."[11] Their habits of life were divided: living as though finance is one thing and mission is another, business on Monday and religion on Sunday.

"The disease of the modern character," writes Berry, "is specialization." It is characterized by the scientist who knows a great deal about stem cells but little of the literature or philosophy that would help her through the moral quandaries of her research, the limits of what she should and shouldn't do. It is by dividing our lives and our concerns that we are able to invest our money in coal companies while giving our charity to fight climate change.

This, for Berry, is the absurdity of modern life. The division of life allows us to avoid the tragedy of our situation and our choices—it enables us to pretend to be in control, to live as gods, while ignoring the obvious examples to the contrary.

To live without division, to live in both the power and the limits of the human life, is to live in hope of comedy in the face of tragedy. Our situation is tragic, whether we ignore it or not, but some hope is in store for those who live into the truth of our givenness and its limits. In Berry's understanding of our givenness, he returns most repeatedly to the Bible and to what is perhaps Shakespeare's greatest tragedy, *King Lear*.

"The whole play is about kindness," writes Berry, "both in the usual sense and in the sense of truth-to-kind, naturalness, or knowing the limits of our specifically *human* nature."[12] Berry finds many of *King Lear*'s deepest lessons in the subplot involving Gloucester, an earl, who in his loyalty to the king in the face of rebellion ends up blinded and seeking to end his life in suicide.

Through a series of altruistic deceptions, Gloucester's son Edgar comes to his blinded father in disguise and prevents his suicide. Gloucester, who has failed in his attempt to kill himself, pushes away the disguised Edgar saying, "Away, and let me die."[13] In reply, after several lines, Edgar speaks to his father saying: "Thy life's a miracle. Speak yet again."[14]

It is this line, Berry writes, "that calls Gloucester back—out of hubris, and the damage and despair that invariably follow—into the properly subordinated human life of grief and joy, where change and redemption are possible."[15] To enter into this place of miracle and mystery, Gloucester is called to give up his attempt to control his life, a control that he sought through suicide.

Such a suicidal despair is at work on many levels in our world, even if the aim is not death. As in the movie *Interstellar*, many are willing to give up on the given world of Earth and to solve its problems through industrial warfare and extreme measures of technology. So, some would attempt to cool our warming planet through "geoengineering," placing mirrors in space or sprays into the atmosphere. "It seems that humans cannot significantly reduce or mitigate the dangers inherent in their use of life by accumulating more information or better theories or by achieving greater predictability or more caution in their scientific and industrial work," writes Berry. "To treat life as less than a miracle is to give up on it."[16]

If we do not want to give up on life, but rather hope to recover our proper place as creatures, "We must learn to live a given life in a given world."[17] To accept this givenness, he says, we must live in "gratitude, and in responsibility of care that is fearful, difficult, and yet pleasing."[18] This fear is not a terror at a malicious world or God, but rather the caution necessary when dealing with a power beyond us, a power that we would be wise not to transgress without proper care or sense of the holy.

In one of his "Sabbath Poems," which Berry writes on occasion when he is enjoying a day of delight and rest in the creation, Berry reflects on the lessons of Gloucester and Edgar in *King Lear,* closing the poem with the line:

We live the given life, and not the planned.[19]

This is a statement of fact, but it is also a statement of grace, if we only accept it as such. To live our lives as given in a world of creatures also given has implications for how we work, the virtues we take up, the relationships we have, the affections we cultivate. How do we live this given life? How do we accept this gift in a world that denies or ignores it? These are the questions we hope to take up in this book with Berry as our guide, our new St. Benedict showing us the ways of life that we need, now, to sustain us.

CHAPTER TWO

Humility

· · · · · · · · · · · · · · · · · ·

COMING TO TERMS WITH REALITY

When I was young, my family took a trip to the Epcot Center at Disney World. Just a few miles from Cape Canaveral, many of its rides were focused on the future, a future always gleaming with the shine of steel and glass, swept clean of dirt or dust. One ride I remember in particular was a tour of the farm of the future, a space where plants grew suspended in the air, nurtured by sprays and artificial lights inside a warehouse. With no sunshine or earth to worry with, it was a model that could have been in Saudi Arabia as much as Florida. It was a farm for anywhere from anywhere.

To the agrarian mind, such a farm is not only unsustainable, but also a kind of lie. It hides us from the truth that our lives are dependent upon the soil and the sun and the plants that can turn both into food. Such a farm represents an attempt to place a basic need fully under human control, but in doing so it separates us from the context in which we are made fully human.

To be human is to be close to the earth. The biblical name for human, *adam*, makes this link because *adam* is made from the *adamah*—a rich life-giving soil. Adam is literally an "earthling," one belonging to and formed from the dirt. In English, the human is, in a similar way, drawn from the humus—our life is dependent, in a most basic way, upon the soil. This is our truth, our reality.

A common response to this fact that we are humus-bound creatures is to try to transcend our earthliness, to free ourselves from our dependence on soil. To the agrarian mind such transcendence is really a transgression of reality and our limits—it is not a heroic enterprise or intelligence but is rather, as Berry puts it, "our old friend hubris, ungodly ignorance disguised as godly arrogance."[1]

Hubris is a Greek term meaning, originally, defiance toward the gods. But it also has in its root a sense of moving up, out of place, of no longer fitting into the proper order of things. Hubris is like those plants at the farm of the future, suspended in the air, roots without soil in which they can be secured. And yet, the reality is that such a "farm of the future" is dependent on fossil fuels, the stored photosynthesis of millennia. The nutrients sprayed on the roots must be taken from nature; they were not synthesized ex nihilo in a lab. Those suspended plants, as genetically modified as they might be, were only the manipulations of a given reality that is far more significant and meaningful and mysterious than any technological enterprise could develop. Even with talk now of "synthetic life," if it is achievable at all, it is only on the pattern of the given life already abundant in the world. Hubris is always poised to learn its opposite the hard way—humility not through reflective wisdom, but by humiliation with a great deal of damage along the way.

Though Berry has called out thinkers such as E.O. Wilson

and Richard Lewontin for their statements typifying what Berry calls "ignorant arrogance," some of his best pictures of what hubris looks like can be found in his novels. In *Jayber Crow*, this hubris is found in Troy Chatham, a star high-school basketball player who wins the affections of Maddie Keith and eventually takes over the farm that her father has carefully stewarded into flourishing. Troy imagines that he is better and smarter than his predecessors on the land. He is arrogant and he is ignorant, and so he goes about using up the farm to feed his ambitions. He plants row crops where his father-in-law knew there would be erosion. He buys big implements that the land and his bank account can't support. Over the course of his life the farm is damaged and Troy is overwhelmed by debt. Because he failed to work in humility, listening to the land, his forebears, and his neighbors, Troy is in the end humiliated though still not humble. And so it goes for too many.

• • •

Hubris is only the most common response to our creaturely condition, but it is not the only choice. "To counter the ignorant use of knowledge and power," says Berry, "we have… only a proper humility."[2] This humility is a going down and acceptance of our limits, but also an embrace of our reality. In humility we turn our eyes to our most basic dependencies, beginning with the humus itself. Cistercian Michael Casey, reflecting on St. Benedict's teaching on humility writes, "The first thrust of humility is to inculcate in us an acceptance that we are of the earth; we are *humus*. To judge ourselves or others from any other perspective is false, and will eventually become destructive."[3]

This going down of humility is not to diminish the human person, but is to bring us in contact with something more essential than mere knowledge: truth. As Bernard of Clairvaux wrote in his classic, *The Steps of Humility and Pride*: "The way is humility, the goal is truth."[4] We can only *know* so much; even with all of the knowledge collected and known, our species is forgetting a great deal at the same time it is advancing knowledge. Our ability to understand is even more limited than our ability to know. As Berry writes, "The mystery surrounding our life probably is not significantly reducible. And so the question of how to act in ignorance is paramount."[5] The problem is that "we are at once limited and unendingly responsible for what we know and do."[6] To learn how to act in the face of such mystery and limits, we need humility. In this way, we can find the truth even in our ignorance.

For Berry, one of the key outgrowths of the virtue of humility is the practice of propriety. "The idea of propriety," he writes, "makes an issue of the fittingness of our conduct to our place or circumstances, even our hopes."[7] Such a fittingness means that our lives are part of a whole and are not complete in themselves, we are each a part of a context outside of which "we cannot speak or act or live."[8]

This context means that our own lives are really never our own: "Our life inescapably affects other lives, which inescapably affect our life."[9] We are entangled and bound up together, not as in a net in which we are trapped, but in a network through which we are nourished and find our health. It is humility that teaches us the good of this entanglement while pride tries to escape our embeddedness, mostly by ignoring it and sometimes by violently wrestling free.

"Propriety is the antithesis of individualism," writes Berry. Propriety is the means by which we "deny that any individual's wish is the ultimate measure of the world."[10] For this reason propriety is concerned with the scale of one's actions. To act with a humble propriety is to recognize that failure is possible and that we should not work beyond our ability to clean up our messes. "When people succeed in profiting on a large scale they succeed for themselves," Berry warns. "When they fail, they fail for many others, sometimes for us all."[11]

This calls to mind the idea that some institutions like banks are "too big to fail," which was of course an ironic statement since they did fail and had to be rescued by the government. One can also look at the BP oil spill or the SoCalGas leak, both of which did tremendous damage to people's lives and livelihoods, not to mention innumerable plants and animals. This damage, as is so often the case with such large-scale wounds, will never fully be accounted for, and those responsible will never be held fully accountable.

These disasters were so beyond our competencies that we not only couldn't understand enough to stop or prevent them, but we are also ignorant of how far and deep the damage runs. Six years after the BP oil spill, its effects are continuing to show up in the Gulf, including a high rate of stillborn dolphins and stranded dolphins with lung problems.[12] We will never fully know the harm done by the spill, but we should always keep in mind that human arrogance was plenty powerful to cause that for which it could not account.

To be humble is to recognize that, in our ignorance, damage is inevitable, and so it is important that the scale of our work doesn't go beyond that to which we can properly respond; we do not, for instance, create systems with leaks that we cannot fix or institutions so large that their risk-taking must be transferred to the citizens of the entire nation.

In his essay "Damage," Berry reflects on this situation of ignorance and propriety on the scale of his own farm. Wanting to provide a permanent water supply on a hillside pasture, Berry hired a man with a bulldozer to dig a small pond on a flat shelf of the hillside. The pond quickly filled and "appeared to be a success." But with a wet fall and winter, the soft ground gave way and a large slice of land above the pond slid into it. "The trouble was the familiar one," wrote Berry, "too much power, too little knowledge."[13]

It was not that Berry hadn't considered the possibilities or had simply gone about having the pond dug without taking care to ask the advice of experts. He talked with the experts, but, as he writes, "No expert knows everything about every place, not even everything about any place."[14] We are fundamentally ignorant in our humanity and so we are bound to make mistakes. The problem in Berry's case, and in our contemporary condition more generally, is that we are able to act with a power that quickly takes us beyond propriety. "A man with a machine and inadequate culture…shakes more than he can hold."[15]

The ability to act in a place without damage, to know enough in our ignorance to have propriety, is guided by culture. "Culture preserves the map and the records of past journeys," writes Berry, "The more local and settled the culture, the better it stays put, the less the damage."[16] Culture connects us to a history, not merely as an assortment of past facts, but as an evaluative means of remembering. Culture enables us to remember and be remembered—to connect with the larger set of human wisdom through which we find a way to live in the truth.

In theological terms, this is called *anamnesis*, the recollection, particularly in the Eucharistic Prayer, in which we draw our own lives back into the tradition of faith and recognize that our worship in each particular service is continuous with the worship that has gone before us. Though Berry doesn't speak in these terms, the work of local culture has this kind of sacramental nature for him. Culture enables the healing by which "the scattered members come together" and "the holy enters the world."[17]

Among the proper lessons of culture is that we remind ourselves of our limits, of our need for community, of our ignorance and the tragic realities of living in such ignorance— lessons, in other words, that help us remember that we are creatures. It is through such recollection, being gathered back to ourselves from the diffuse ambitions that draw us away from our roots, that we are able to begin to heal the damage done to the world and ourselves. "The task of healing," writes Berry, "is to respect oneself as a creature, no more and no less."[18]

Humility, by helping to return us to the integrity of our humanity, which involves an acceptance of our particularly human creatureliness, also helps to make our lives more coherent, more integrated. "The more coherent one becomes within oneself as a creature," writes Berry, "the more fully one enters into the communion of all creatures."[19] It is by humility then that we join the membership of creation in acceptance that we are a part of the world rather than an individual struggling against it. There is grace and community for us, if only we would accept the gift of our givenness.

There is a restfulness in this acceptance of our limited lives. When we move low, back toward the soil from which we can learn the lessons of our true humanity, we are able to enter a kind of peace. Humility is not about struggle or diminishment but rather is the relief that we are not God, that we are mere creatures. Berry gives voice to this truth in one of his most popular poems, "The Peace of Wild Things":

> When despair for the world grows in me
> and I wake in the night at the least sound
> in fear of what my life and my children's lives may be,
> I go and lie down where the wood drake
> rests in his beauty on the water, and the great heron feeds.
> I come into the peace of wild things
> who do not tax their lives with forethought
> of grief. I come into the presence of still water.
> And I feel above me the day-blind stars
> waiting with their light. For a time
> I rest in the grace of the world, and am free.[20]

Berry, in seeking and finding the "grace of the world," is following a thread of insight running from Psalm 23 to the Sermon on the Mount where Jesus calls us to live as sparrows and lilies, which is to say, to rest in the blessings of our givenness. To accept that we are creatures is to live into a kind of peace at the base of the world.

St. Augustine writes, in the *City of God*, that "the peace of all things is the tranquility of order" (Book XIX, Ch. 13). By this he means that things are at peace when they are where they should be, being what they should be. The creature lives as a creature, the human as a human, God as God, and all are in proper relationship with one another.

This rest and peace are broken by disordered desires, by pride that is unsettled in its place. As Berry writes, "it is pride that lies awake in the night with its desire and its grief."[21] The solution is to live with a proper ordering of our lives. In a play on the structure of a sentence, Berry writes in his essay "Healing": "Order is the only possibility of rest." Then at the close of the essay he writes, "Order is only the possibility of rest." The two are tied together—peace and order—to be at rest is to fit in the place you are meant to be, to accept and work well within the confines of creatureliness.

Berry's "The Peace of Wild Things," though it makes an allusion to Psalm 23, also calls to mind another great psalm on humility, Psalm 131:

O Lord, my heart is not lifted up,
  my eyes are not raised too high;
I do not occupy myself with things
  too great and too marvelous for me.
But I have calmed and quieted my soul,
  like a weaned child with its mother;
  my soul is like the weaned child that is with me.
O Israel, hope in the Lord
  from this time on and forevermore. (English Standard Version)

The psalmist calls on us to accept our ignorance, to not occupy ourselves with things too great for us, but rather to rest in God like a child with its mother. This is the peace Berry finds in the grace of the world, which is the acceptance of our place as creatures.

Many may react against both Berry and Psalm 131 that these calls toward the acceptance of limits, of not occupying ourselves with things beyond ourselves, lends to a quelling of human knowledge and advancement. Would we have antibiotics if we didn't have scientists who were willing to push the limits of knowledge? What if, to give a favored example of the promoters of scientific knowledge, Galileo had not challenged the accepted earth-centered view of his time?

Humility must demand that we are open to revising our ideas when new information comes. But what Berry, and I believe the psalmist, are warning against is a seeking of knowledge that ignores the formal restraints of our creatureliness. One need not look far to see that there are scientists everywhere looking to significantly alter parts of our world in ways that fundamentally violate the relationships that have been integral from the beginning of the creation. Some are even seeking means to create life "from scratch," rather than adapting given forms within their limits. Such acts are bound to lead toward destruction.[22] Such knowledge is aimed at godlike power rather than creaturely art and understanding.

"We live and prosper by form, which is the power of creatures and artifacts to be made whole within their proper limits," writes Berry.[23] To be humble, seeking to live well in this dirt-dependent life, is a path toward wholeness and fulfillment and creativity. It is within the bounds of form, which must have boundaries and limits, that "we reunite science and art."[24] Limits are not then the closure of creativity, but rather an invitation toward the flourishing exercise of our human understanding. As Berry puts it, "our human and earthly limits, properly understood, are not confinements but rather inducements to formal elaboration and elegance, to *fullness* of relationship and meaning."[25]

To be humble, to accept our limits, is to find the grounding for our becoming fulfilled. It is a striving against those limits that has led to much misery and a great deal of destruction, including the wide-scale erosion of the very soil we are supposed to move toward in our lowliness. What if we could stop, breathe in our God-given breath, live our given lives in the forms through which we can find our fullness?

I often think of those plants I saw in the farm of the future, suspended in the air. My memory of them carries not a sense of their buoyancy, airborne though they were, but of their weight. How heavy those plants were on the earth—how costly to the ecosystems on which they were dependent and from which they were divided. How much lighter it would have been for those plants to have found their flourishing in the soil from which they could rise on sunshine and humus, bourn up from the dirt and held close by gravity:

> The garden delves no deeper than its roots
> And lifts no higher than its leaves and fruits.[26]

So writes Berry of this path of humility, the path toward the truthful lives that admit that God is God and we are God's creatures. It is a path that finds in gravity a gift that unburdens us through the life of love.

CHAPTER THREE

Love

IT ALL TURNS ON AFFECTION

When I was a boy, my family lived for a time in a suburban neighborhood. Despite the lawns and blacktop, there was a small patch of woods behind our house—five acres or so—where I spent long hours exploring and playing. I knew those woods deeply—where the possum's den was and the patches of moss that made for a good pillow, where a Chuck-will's-widow bird slept, and the creek pools in which songbirds bathed. I loved the woods and all the creatures that lived in them.

One day I went on a walk along the creek and saw an oil slick spreading over the water. Someone had poured large quantities of used motor oil down a storm drain and it had ended up in this creek at the center of the woods I knew and loved. I was outraged at the pollution and destruction of this place because, in some way, I sensed that something holy had been defiled. I understood, even as a boy, the sentiment expressed by Berry: "There are no unsacred places; / there are only sacred places / and desecrated places."[1] Desecration was just what had happened there.

My love moved my outrage, which then moved my action—I looked in the phone book and called the Environmental Protection Agency. An inspector came, gracious to take the call for what I'm sure was a comparatively small environmental crime. He patiently followed me to see the oil slick and dead birds, and listened as I told him my suspicion that a body builder up the street, always working on his friends' cars, was the perpetrator. The EPA inspector offered him a warning, but could do nothing more given the lack of clear evidence. No more oil spills happened while I lived there.

I begin with this anecdote because what drove my action, what animated and directed it, was love. Over those many mornings and evenings, those long hours being in the place, I had come to love it and, because I loved it, I also defended it as best I could as a young boy.

To be a human creature, a person that somehow bears the image of God, means that love is properly at our core. When we move in proper relation to the world we move with affection. And it is this affection that guides our action and directs the boundaries of our limits.

Affection is a key theme in Berry's work and with it the metaphors of marriage and divorce. Love can never be general or abstract—it is only concrete and particular. What we know of other loves we know by analogy because as a creature I must live in the limits of my love. I cannot love forests in general any more than I can love people in general. As the essayist Charles D'Ambrosio has put it, "If you can love abstractly, you're only a bad day away from hating abstractly."[2] For love to work, it must be anchored in the particular or else it is likely to simply float along with the changing currents of emotion.

The deeper my love the more particular it becomes and the more limited in scope. It is only through such particulars that we can come to save the creation. God may love the world, but we live into God's image by reflecting such love on a proper scale—among particular places and people. We live into our love when we love our neighbors and, thus necessarily, our neighborhood.

Some might complain, and some have, that such a vision is provincial—that in a global age we need to take up the call to be citizens of the world and expand our moral vision to include the whole of it. Some people also reject monogamous marriage as the standard of love. In both cases, human and ecological wreckage typically ensue because such ideas deny the authentic possibility and practice of human love, which must always be to scale and must always be practiced with fidelity. A global ethic is likely to do no better than the global economy in naming and valuing what is truly good and lovely in the world. Love can begin in general, in the instinctual drives, but it must arrive at home if it is to last. Berry writes: "One who returns home—to one's marriage and household and place in the world—desiring anew what was previously chosen, is neither the world's stranger nor its prisoner, but is at once in place and free."[3] Freedom then comes not from escaping the bonds of love, but by returning to see that they are not bonds at all.

Berry takes up this tension between the general and the particular in relationship with the desire to care for the "planet." "Our understandable wish to preserve the planet must somehow be reduced to the scale of [human] competence," writes Berry, "that is, to the wish to preserve all its humble households and neighborhoods."[4] When we reach beyond this human scale we have a tendency to subvert the very end we are seeking to accomplish. This is how, for instance, Adam Werbach, a former head of the Sierra Club, ended up working for Wal-Mart. He came to believe that it was more *effective* to "green" the world's largest retailer than to fundamentally challenge the consumerist society of which such a company is a part.

The radical Catholic priest and social critic Ivan Illich recognized this problem as one at the core of modern history. For Illich, modernity arose out of a desire to codify and institutionalize the call to love our neighbor, a reality that always had a contingent aspect to it. As Jesus illustrated in the parable of the Good Samaritan, loving our neighbor means loving those we happen upon. There was a kind of freedom in this call, but as Illich writes, "The Western Church, in its earnest effort to institutionalize this freedom, has tended to transform supreme folly first into desirable duty, and then into legislated duty."[5] In other words, where the Good Samaritan emphasizes the chance encounter and responsiveness of the Samaritan who acts with compassion, Western civilization, first through the church and then the state, has tried to codify this action rooted in affection into an action rooted in duty.

As the Catholic philosopher Charles Taylor writes reflecting on Illich's work: "Ours is a civilization concerned to relieve suffering and enhance human well-being, on a universal scale unprecedented in history, and which at the same time threatens to imprison us in forms that can turn alien and dehumanizing."[6] This is just the kind of problem that Berry is addressing—there can be no effective love for the environment or even the creation in general. Our love, if it is authentic, is going to necessarily be particular.

Drawing from the Sermon on the Mount and the Gospel of Matthew (chapter 25), Berry reflects on this kind of love. "Love is never abstract," writes Berry. "It does not adhere to universe or the planet or the nation or the institution or the profession, but to the singular sparrows of the street, the lilies of the field, 'the least of these my brethren.'"[7]

In order to be particular love must then also be partial and limited. To love involves renunciation on the part of love and because of love. The creation itself is the result of such a limiting. As the French philosopher and mystic Simone Weil put it:

> On God's part creation is not an act of self-expansion but of restraint and renunciation. God and all his creatures are less than God alone. God accepted this diminution. He emptied a part of his being from himself.... God permitted the existence of things distinct from himself and worth infinitely less than himself. By this creative act he denied himself, as Christ has told us to deny ourselves. God denied himself for our sakes in order to give us the possibility of denying ourselves for him.[8]

If we are to love as God has loved us, then our lives must involve renunciation so that we can make room for the rest of the creation.

Just as love in a family requires the limits of marriage and then the limits necessary for the healthy raising of children, so we must learn to live more limited lives out of love for our places and all of the creatures that live in them. This is limit so that we can have expansion; just as God limits Godself for the sake of the world, we must limit our power and the space our lives take up in the world so that other creatures may have room to flourish. In order to enact this love, we must reorient our desires toward those who guide our limits. As Francis de Sales wrote "Love the poor and love poverty, for it is by such love that we become truly poor. As the Scripture says, we become like the things we love."[9]

This is echoed by Berry when he writes, "We must achieve the character and acquire the skills to live much poorer than we do."[10] Such character comes from a change in our affections. We can only achieve the character necessary to limit our lives so that the creation might flourish if we have cultivated the kind of love for God and the creation that requires such limits.

We are led to think by the culture of consumerism that such limits are negative, that they will hinder our potential and our fulfillment, but quite the opposite is true. Because proper limits are born in affection, they lead inevitably to pleasure because, as Berry writes, "pleasure is, so to speak, affection in action."[11]

Pleasure is at the heart of divine affection. God loves the world and has pleasure in its existence. Berry reflects on this by looking at Revelation 4:11 where God is praised: "For thou hast created all things, and for thy pleasure they are and were created" (King James Version). Berry writes that this "passage suggests...that our truest and profoundest religious experience may be the simple, unasking pleasure in the existence of other creatures that is possible to humans."[12] It is in these pleasures that we become most human, for "in these pleasures...we possess the likeness of God that is spoken of in Genesis."[13] We are in God's likeness in the world, not through our rationality or profound creativity, but through our love and our pleasure in the world.

But again, this isn't the pleasure of consumerism—what Berry calls the pleasure of the one-night stand—"it was nice to know you but don't tell me your name." Instead this is the pleasure born of sustained affection, of fidelity. "The primary motive for good care and good use is always going to be affection," writes Berry, "because affection involves us entirely."[14] To love we must submit ourselves to the beloved, we must be subject to our subject as Berry often says.

Berry has expressed this through the metaphor of marriage, suggesting that, in a way, our relationship with a local land-scape must be like that of a marriage. It requires us to stay through the ups and downs of life so that the deeper goods and harder pleasures can come. It also requires a context, a place in which love can find a body. Affection and love are always incarnational for Berry; they work from what is known. "Love proposes the work of settled households and communities," writes Berry, "whose innovations come about in response to immediate needs and immediate conditions."[15] This is exhibited particularly well in Berry's novel *Hannah Coulter*, in which the title character's marriage to Nathan Coulter coincides with the establishment of their farm.

Describing that farm, she reflects on the ways it became an embodiment of their life together. She says, describing the place, "what I see always, is the pattern of our life here that made and kept it as you see it now.... A lifetime's knowledge shimmers on the face of the land in the mind of a person who knows."[16] It is the land, this place, which retains the physical memory of their life together.

Most of us can hardly hope for such an embodiment of our common lives, our affections familial or otherwise. My own places are spread over several states. My wife and I have nowhere that embodies our life together. And Berry knows this is a reality for many of his readers, even as it was a reality for Berry's own post-college years. What he is telling us, though, is that love must be embodied, it must be made manifest in a common life that is not isolated but is in community. For love to work, it must eventually settle down and stay.

This stable love is not simply the public affection of family life or the non-sexual varieties of love such as agape. The deep sort of love that will save the world involves the intimate, sexual kind of love as well. In one of his best known essays, "Sex, Economy, Freedom, and Community" Berry writes that "Sexual love is the heart of community life. Sexual love is the force that in our bodily life connects us most intimately to the Creation, to the fertility of the world, to farming and the care of animals. It brings us into the dance that holds the community together and joins it to its place."[17]

It is this communal nature of love that makes marriage possible and critical. "Lovers must not…live for themselves alone," writes Berry, "They must finally turn from their gaze at one another and back toward the community."[18] In Christian marriage, the wedding is properly celebrated in a church—it is not a private spectacle but rather a public affirmation that the community agrees to uphold, enabling the couple to embark on a life they cannot even imagine or yet understand.

The act of marriage is also a giving that escapes the economy of exchange. "[L]overs, pledging themselves to one another 'until death,' are giving themselves away, and they are joined by this as no law or contract could ever join them."[19] Their gift of love to each other represents the gift of love that is at the heart of the whole community. "If the community cannot protect this giving," Berry writes, "it cannot protect anything."[20] When community is collapsed into the market, then the market will sell it to the highest or most expedient bidder. Love and community, as gifts, must stand outside of such economies of exchange.

• • •

That affection is formed and expressed in a particular context is made evident in another way in Berry's short story "Fidelity." In the story Burley Coulter, an old man who in his younger days was renowned as a coon hunter, fisherman, and all around independent man, is in the hospital dying. He is a person who lived in the Port William Membership, the community of living and dead, human and animal, and inanimate realities that make up the whole of the place in and around Port William, Kentucky— the fictional community at the heart of Berry's short stories, novels, and even some of his poetry.

In the story, we find Burley Coulter removed from that community in which his life was meaningful, hooked up to tubes and machines in the sterile world of the hospital. His son, Danny, goes to visit his father, now in a coma, in the hospital. Danny, writes Berry, "found the old body still as it had been, a mere passive addition to the complicated machines that kept it minimally alive."[21] Danny feels regret for having taken his father into the hospital: "Loving him, wanting to help him, they had given him over to 'the best of modern medical care'—which meant, as they now saw, that they had abandoned him."[22]

As the story continues, Danny thinks of the wholeness his father found in his place. "In love Burley had assumed many responsibilities," writes Berry. "In love and responsibility, as everyone must, he had acquired his griefs and losses, guilts and sorrows. Sometimes, under the burden of these, he sought the freedom of solitude in the woods."[23] It was there that Burley became again who he was; it was in the woods of his place that he was recollected as a person. "When he returned," Berry writes, "he would be smiling, at ease and quiet, as if his mind just fit within his body."[24] It is this return to his place of wholeness that Danny wants for his father, and so he breaks him out of the hospital.

The police treat the disappearance as a kidnapping, and the investigator in the case, Kyle Bode, travels around the Port William community in search of Danny and Burley. At every turn, the community, well aware of the situation, cover for Danny and obstruct Bode's investigation.

The contrast between the kind of settled love found in Port William and manifest in Danny's love for his father is in stark contrast to Bode's own life and loves. Bode is a man who has lived for individual freedom, and that freedom has been the opposite of the fidelity that drove Burley to assume "many responsibilities" out of love. When Bode's second wife left him, Berry writes: "He knew that she had not left him because she was dissatisfied with him but because she was not able to be satisfied for very long with anything.... He, too, was dissatisfied; he could not see what he had because he was always looking around for something else that he thought he wanted. And so perhaps it was out of mutual dissatisfaction that their divorce had come, and now they were free."[25] Free, but also forgotten.

Burley dies, eventually, and Danny buries him in the woods of his home place. For Bode this is a crime, for Danny it is love.

Detective Bode represents the way of abstract "freedom"—a way marked by the *feelings* of love rooted in the self's fleeting satisfactions and fulfillments. Danny represents the way of fidelity, and so in his desire and effort to help his father die at home, he is involved in the *practice* of love—"trust, patience, respect, mutual help, forgiveness."[26] Danny, taking his father home, burying him in the woods his father loved, is giving body to the person who was disappearing in the midst of systems and machines, but remembered in the Port William membership.

In his act of returning his father to his farm, Danny is embodying love—making it concrete and placed. He is unifying, reuniting, bringing together so that there might be some hope of wholeness. This is what love does.

In his essay *It All Turns on Affection*, Berry quotes English philosopher and geometer, Keith Critchlows: "The human mind takes apart with its analytic habits of reasoning but the human heart puts things together because it loves them." This unity is not something any person or place or affection accomplishes in itself. It is a unity born from common givenness and the affection that lives in that givenness.

There is a remarkable stanza in Berry's long poem *The Country of Marriage* that expresses the common gift within which love properly lives:

Our bond is no little economy based on the exchange
of my love and work for yours, so much for so much
of an expendable fund. We don't know what its limits are—
that puts us in the dark. We are more together
than we know, how else could we keep on discovering
we are more together than we thought?

You are the known way leading always to the unknown,
and you are the known place to which the unknown is always
leading me back. More blessed in you than I know,
I possess nothing worthy to give you, nothing
not belittled by my saying that I possess it.
Even an hour of love is a moral predicament, a blessing
a man may be hard up to be worthy of. He can only
accept it, as a plant accepts from all the bounty of the light
enough to live, and then accepts the dark,
passing unencumbered back to the earth, as I
have fallen time and again from the great strength
of my desire, helpless, into your arms.[27]

Berry here expresses the love of marriage, as we have discussed it—a mystery in which known leads to unknown, a place where exchange is impossible because value is beyond calculation. It is given and so it presents the "moral predicament" of what to do with the gift. Possess it? Hold on to it? The answer can only be, as with any real gift, "accept it." In such an acceptance we embrace life and death, limits and blessing, with the knowledge that what will hold our loves in place is not ultimately ourselves, but those from whom and to which we are given.

CHAPTER FOUR

· · ·

Economics

· · · · · · · · · · · · · · · · ·

HOME AND CARE IN THE KINGDOM OF GOD

The meadowlarks trill from the fence posts, their breasts bright with yellow, offset by a stark black V in the middle. Up the hill, there is a stand of timber, uncut in the last century, its older members too large for an embrace. Across the grass, sheep move, their heads down to the spring shoots of grass, roots running into the soil made by a millennium of decay. The farmhouse is white, two stories with a porch across the front. A barn sits below, near the river where catfish lurk in the deep and green herons stalk spawning brim in the shallows.

How can we account for such a place? There are prices that can be applied—a price per acre of land, a price per board foot of timber, per pound of flesh, etc. But would such prices name the real value? Would an economy built around such an accounting be in any way a true economy? Would such prices help retain or at least not violate the value for which that they could not account?

Among the given, the created, the answer must be "no." In the world called "good" from its beginning, whose blessing is built into its fabric, any economy that would propose to be complete with the assignment of a market price would be a lie.

What kind of economy would be large enough to claim all that is truly valuable? It was this question that Wendell Berry and his friend, the agrarian geneticists and plant breeder Wes Jackson, took up one day in conversation. As recounted in his essay, "Two Economies," Berry offered that perhaps an energy economy would be better than a money economy because it would include more in its scope, but Jackson rejected the proposal. Such an economy would still be too small. Frustrated, Berry asked what economy would be large enough, and Jackson replied—"The Kingdom of God."

Berry goes on to explore what such an economy of the Kingdom of God would look like, calling it, alternatively, the "Great Economy." Such a comprehensive economy is one defined by its inclusion—a scope of accounting where "the fall of every sparrow is a significant event." The Kingdom of God is a place where all is not only included but connected, whether we know it or not. It is a whole and it is orderly, but our understanding cannot comprehend it. It comprehends us, to be our subject we must recognize first that we are subject to it. We cannot know all of the creatures included in this kingdom or "the whole pattern or order by which it contains them."[1]

Our own economies, which are invariably within the Great Economy, must begin from this place of ignorance, the admittance that any accounting we give is tentative. We must act humbly and carefully, understanding that consequences are in store for those who violate the order of the Great Economy, a reality we can violate simply by refusing to account for it.

We must, Berry acknowledges and advocates, work on the scale of small economies—economies in which we can make some sense of the whole and make some accounting of value. These economies must, however, exist acknowledging that they are within the greater economy of the whole.

Berry's understanding of economy depends upon the word's roots in the Greek: *oikos* and *nomos*. *Oikos*, a word which is also the root for *ecology*, is a term that means household. *Nomos* means management or ordering, a rule or law. "Economy in its original—and I think proper sense—refers to household management," Berry writes, "By extension it refers to the husbanding of all the goods by which we live."[2]

The whole of the creation is in a way the household of God, "the outermost house," as the writer Henry Beston put it. It is the domain of God's ordering and God's concerns within it reach beyond those of the human order. We see this in the biblical book of Job, where God responds to Job's questions with an accounting of the parts of creation that are within God's concern but well outside of any human purpose or accounting. Job is, in effect, put in his place, and he finds the recovery of right perspective as a kind of liberation.

That our own households and their ordering are within God's household changes how we act. Like a child's room within a family house, there are certain freedoms, but also a great many limits to what can be done by the child within her small kingdom. The Great Economy has priority and offers definition to any small economy that is within it.

The pattern for any small economy must be the Great Economy, and though it cannot comprehend the great economy, it can work in analog to it. The measure of any small economy is the degree to which it can subsist within and imitate the great economy.

In working on this level, it must acknowledge that, though it can "evaluate and distribute and preserve things of value," no human economy can "make value." The small economy must then be an economy of "husbanding the goods by which we live."[3] Our human economies properly manage what they receive and live under the rule of that given value. The problem is that we do not tend to keep our households in analog to the Kingdom of God. "The 'environmental crisis,'" writes Berry, "has happened because the human household or economy is in conflict at almost every point with the household of nature."[4]

That we do not now live in such an economy is easy enough to see. We propose to make value through a contrived market and exclude from our accounting all that is valuable outside of the market, those things that can never have a price. How else could we power our lights with coal extracted by blasting apart entire mountains, leaving landscapes that will never again be whole? Berry contrasts the two possibilities for these small economies that typify the human systems of household management under the names "agrarian" and "industrial." It is the industrial economy that tends to go by the name "economy." It is what is typically traded on the market and measured by the Gross Domestic Product.

The industrial economy arose with the Industrial Revolution, but its vision extends beyond it both before the Enlightenment and after the economy that some would call "post-industrial."[5]

Berry writes that the "way of Industrialism is the way of the machine." By this he means that industrialism not only relies on and makes use of machines, but that it takes the machine to be "an explanation of the world and of life."[6]

Under industrialism, the whole of creation, and by extension human lives, become subject to the metaphor of the machine and are judged by machine values. Animal life, which agrarianism has always understood as demanding respectful and humane treatment, is transformed in the industrial mind into a "protein solution." These animals, which Psalm 104 says gain their life from the spirit of God, are treated as widgets in a factory—their disease and defecation the only evidence that they are living beings.

Berry believes, following the poet William Blake, that such economies are satanic. Writing in the midst of the Industrial Revolution in England, Blake spoke of the "dark satanic mills" working with "satanic wheels" which turned in opposition to the great wheel of all creation. Instead of the small economy turning within the large economy, the mill works in destructive independence (even though its independence is merely its failure to account properly for what it has received or stolen from the Great Economy).

This industrial economy is satanic because it moves against our lives as gifts among the wider gifts of creation. In this economy we began to see ourselves as "not a part of or a member of creation, but as outside it and opposed to it."[7] This is a kind of pride and at its root is a value-blindness. As Dietrich von Hildebrand says, this is a satanic pride that fears values "as a menace to his supreme glory derived from his autonomous selfhood."[8] In such pride, we cannot see anything but our own vision of goodness. The value of the world becomes defined only by our measure—"man is the measure of all things."

Recognizing no value in creation apart from itself, the industrial economy relates to the world through a mode that Naomi Klein has called extractivism. As Berry writes, "The invariable mode [of the industrial economy's] relation both to nature and to human culture is that of mining."[9] Mining takes resources from the land and uses them up. In the case of the coal that is mined in Berry's home state of Kentucky, the land is literally burned up. Such an economy produces, in addition to whatever gains it makes, a great deal of pollution and waste—pollution and waste that are rarely accounted for in part or whole.

The extractive economy wastes people as well as the creation. The industrial economy makes a waste of everything it touches. As Berry writes, "If we wish to correct this economy, we must be careful to understand and demonstrate how much waste of human life is involved in our waste of the material goods of creation."[10] This waste is not only the lives that are used up and cast aside. The industrial economy also increases dependence upon centralized industries to supply basic goods. As Berry writes, "much of the litter that now defaces our country is fairly directly caused by the massive secession or exclusion of most of our people from active participation in the food economy... the more dependent we become on the *industries* of eating and drinking the more waste we are going to produce."[11]

This also brings us to the idea of proxies, a key aspect of Berry's economics. Proxies are the ways in which we allow others to do things *for* us or on our behalf. One of the problems of the industrial economy and its inevitable move toward a consumer economy "is that most people in the 'developed' world have given proxies to the corporations to produce and provide *all* of their food, clothing, and shelter." Beyond these basic human needs, Berry writes that, "Moreover, [people] are rapidly increasing their proxies to corporations or governments to provide entertainment, education, child care, care of the sick and the elderly, and many other kinds of 'service' that were once carried on informally and inexpensively by individuals or households or communities."[12]

The problem with such proxies is that they remove us from the practices by which we might properly care for one another and for the whole of creation. "A change of heart or of values without a *practice* is only another pointless luxury of a passively consumptive way of life," writes Berry (emphasis mine).[13] Without some concrete form by which we manage our household or care for the goods of creation, we become bystanders to the destruction of creation, a destruction we have enacted by proxy. "We have an 'environmental crisis,'" writes Berry, "because *we* have consented to an economy in which by eating, drinking, working, resting, traveling, and enjoying ourselves we are destroying the natural, the God-given, world."[14]

There *is* a choice involved here. Though we are all implicated in the fabric of the Industrial economy, there are alternatives available, different ways of existing in relation to the goods of the world. This brings us to agrarianism—the form of economy Berry advocates.

"The fundamental difference between Industrialism and agrarianism is this," writes Berry: "Whereas Industrialism is a way of thought based on monetary capital and technology, agrarianism is a way of thought based on land."[15] To begin with land is to begin with the fundamental gifts of creation, it is to measure and expand human work with this gift from our first vocation—to till and keep the garden (Genesis 2). While industrialism holds as its aspirational model the capitalist, "self-made" and world making man, agrarianism holds up the model of the careful farmer as its ideal. Farming, in the agrarian sense, is "the proper use and care of an immeasurable gift."[16]

That land is immeasurable and a gift is impossible for the industrial mind to recognize. Land, for the industrialist, is something that can be measured and priced. It has no value outside of the value that it serves as a resource. If the market for a food or forest grown from the land is too low, then even the land itself can go up for sale.

I once knew a farmer who was literally mining the rich, river-bottom topsoil from his farm. "My soil's worth more than anything I can grow out of it," he said. Such a statement is true in the industrial and agrarian understanding, but it means very different things. For the industrialist, as in the case of this farmer, it meant loading up the soil in dump trucks and shipping it away. For the agrarian, the soil is worth more than anything that can be raised from it because the soil is very close to the source of life. It is the gift that makes sustained life in a place possible. To sell it, or let it run off down the river, is like giving away a child, or owning another human being. Indeed, the slave-holding plantation and the factory farm are not far apart and are historically linked. Both seek to profit from the exploitation of that which no one can properly own or put a price to. Since the time of slavery, there has been a conflict between small-holders who sought to live from the land and plantation owners who sought to exploit it.

The agrarian economy is centered, instead, on living within a human scale focused foremost on fulfilling its basic needs rather than profits and export. As Berry writes, "An agrarian economy is always a subsistence economy before it is a market economy. The center of an agrarian farm is the household."[17]

An agrarian's work and economy is guided by the sustaining of life in the careful management of resources from an immeasurable gift. This can be known away from the farm, but it is in working with the landscape of a farm or forest that one can most directly witness the connections between subsistence and gift. It is the task of those who do not farm to put themselves in as close a relationship with farmers as possible; this also goes for those who use any other product, whether it be forest products such as furniture or the fiber for clothes. Doing more for ourselves will help us engage in the practices of the agrarianism that starts from the gift of good land.

Such practices are rooted in the difficult and often tragic position we find ourselves in in relationship to the gifts of creation. As Berry writes, "Our life of need and work forces us inescapably to use in time things belonging to eternity, and to assign finite values to things already recognized as infinitely valuable."[18] This is a reality we must approach, as we approach all things greater than ourselves and beyond ourselves, with fear and trembling. The virtues with which we must work are those of "prudence, humility, good work, propriety of scale." We must practice "the complex responsibilities of caretaking and giving-back that we mean by 'stewardship.'"[19]

This stewardship represents the careful work of subsistence, of living from a small piece of land through a love of it and a sense of its abundance, an abundance that "comes from the experienced possibility of frugality and renewal within limits."[20] Berry holds up for us the Latin poet Virgil's example, in his Fourth Georgic, of an old squatter who made a life from "An acre or two of land that no one wanted" and yet, "By planning here and there among the scrub / Cabbages or white lilies and verbena...fancied himself a king / In wealth, and coming home late in the evening / Loaded his board with unbought delicacies."[21]

To have land is then the greatest need, above that of providing some factory or industry for economic development. For the agrarian, the thing most needful is to have a little space by which one can subsist and perhaps, as in Virgil's poem, live in a kind of wealth. This reality can be understood by its negative: without land, you have "no food, no shelter, no warmth, no freedom, no life." It is for this reason that Berry says, "We know that all economies begin to lie as soon as they assign a fixed value to land."[22]

Subsistence as the standard protects the idea of property from one in which the accrual of too much of it is valorized. The agrarian is to work within limits, on a limited scale, in a limited place. It is by these limits that the agrarian is then able to exercise the economy that is the "primary vocation and responsibility of every one of us." This economy is created through "the *arts* of adapting kindly the many human households to the earth's many ecosystems and human neighborhoods."[23]

It is in light of these concerns that Berry has advocated, throughout his life, the development of local economies, particularly local food economies. It should be said, however, that food economies are simply the most basic first step for Berry's larger vision of an economy scaled to proper human life—a life in which the human household might be managed without violating (and eventually facing penalties) the Great Economy, the Kingdom of God.

In addition to subsistence, Berry says that the "idea of a local economy" rests on the "*practice* of neighborhood."[24] Such a practice, to be viable, requires that "neighbors ask themselves what they can do or provide for one another" and that "they find answers that they and their place can afford." This means that no one in a community will necessarily become rich, though many will be "prosperous," but neither will many become poor.

In Berry's novel *Jayber Crow*, this principle is exhibited by the way the town ensures that its bachelor barber is taken care of. His work is good, his prices are what can be afforded by the farmers and small business people that come by, and they in turn show up on a regular basis for their haircuts. The town takes care of its own and so it ensures that the town itself will survive.

At this writing, many small towns in my home state of Arkansas are facing a challenge due to choices made in the opposite direction. Many Arkansas communities welcomed the chain discount store Wal-Mart and chose, through that commerce, to export their money from the community. Now Wal-Mart, upon which these towns have become dependent for goods and employment, has decided to close many of the lower volume stores. The result is that the towns, whose local businesses were overwhelmed by the economic scale of Wal-Mart, are now left with nothing. The people living in these places must now go further for their goods, and thus be further removed from the scale upon which proper care is possible.

* * *

Perhaps Berry's greatest model for a thriving local economy, existing not in fiction or memory, but one that can still be experienced and witnessed is to be found among the Amish. Berry has been in conversation with these communities over many years and has developed a particular friendship with Amish bishop, writer, and farmer, David Klein.

"We live by mercy, if we live" writes Berry, in his poem "Amish Economy," going on to contrast it with the industrial economy where, in the formulation of Berry's friend Maury Telleen, "cost + greed – fear = price." In such an economy:

> The need to balance greed and fear
> Affords no stopping place, no rest,
> And need increases as we fail.

The Amish, however, care for their neighborhood and are thus able to rest within it. As Berry closes the poem:

> But now, in summer dusk, a man
> Whose hair and beard curl like spring ferns
> Sits under the yard trees, at rest,
> His smallest daughter on his lap.
> This is because he rose at dawn,
> Cared for his own, helped his neighbors,
> Worked much, spent little, kept his peace.[25]

It is such an economy, rooted in analog to the "Great Economy," that provides our best hope of living into the fullness of God's gifts, the immeasurable value for which we can give no account and no other proper response than gratitude.

CHAPTER FIVE

Work

TILLING AND KEEPING THE CREATION

In the beginning, God made a garden, rich with compost and humus, a black loam that smelled of dawn. Seeds began sprouting in this soil; trees' roots wound deep within it as their branches reached toward the sun; grass, clover, and forbs of every kind spread over the earth in a green and golden carpet. God took some of this dirt, made muddy with dew, and formed a creature from it—a body of soil. Bending down, God breathed spirit, *animus*, into the earth so that it became an *animal*—a living thing. And God gave this animal something different from the others—a purpose, a call, an invitation to join God in moving the creation toward its flourishing. God put this humus-man, this human, in the garden and gave it a call—a vocation. God put the human in a place cultivated toward its fullness— a garden—and called the human to "cultivate it and keep it" (Genesis 2:15), to bring it to life and yet to respect its integrity.

This is Genesis 2 in a loose Midrash form, an interpretive retelling meant to draw out the implicit truths of the passage. Those truths here are that we are made from the earth and bound to it, not only in our source of bodily life, but also in our vocation. Our work as human creatures is to serve and preserve the creation so that it can flourish. We are to make use of the world, as all creatures must, through metabolism and waste, but our use also has an end that stretches beyond our own need. To be a human creature in the fullest sense means that we should answer the call to "till and to keep" the garden.

What this vocation means in our own time is a question with which we must struggle. The Hebrew verb translated as "till" in Genesis 2:15 is one that can also mean "to serve." The call to till can then have a broader meaning of "serving" the needs and life of the garden which is the cultivated space of the creation. The second part of the call to "keep" the garden points toward the need to preserve the integrity of creation. It is a call to direct our service within the given integrity of creation rather than giving into the common human desire for manipulation beyond that integrity through enhancements such as genetic engineering —a process whose aims are generally short sighted and move humanity from the role of keeper into the role of creator.

The question of what the call to serve and keep the creation means in our own time is also complicated by the reality that our occupations and economy are, for good or ill, more complicated than simply being farmers. We wouldn't want to argue, for instance, that writing is a worthless labor simply because it involves no seeds. It is possible, however, to find in this original human vocation a standard by which my writing can be questioned. Is it serving the creation? Is it working toward its continued integrity? This is a standard, also, that would question any understanding of work and economy that diminishes this idea of vocation.

• • •

The question of work has been a central one in Berry's writing. It is in work that we find the test of our relationship to the creation because work is the question of how we will use the creation. For Berry, work done well brings us into a wholeness and cooperation with the creation in which we can find health. Bad work destroys the connections that make life possible.

For Berry good work is like a prayer—it is an act of both gratitude and return. Good work accepts the gifts of creation and uses those gifts to further their givenness. There are seeds that lie for decades in the soil, waiting for the right conditions before springing to life. Good work is that which creates the conditions for such life to burst forth from the whole of the creation.

The Benedictine formula—to work and to pray—has always had within it the recognition that good work is prayer and that prayer is work, both are tasks that can be properly moved toward being in communion with our creator. The kind of work Berry calls for is then work that will pray, and it doesn't take much looking in our economy to see that in fact there is a great deal of work that doesn't pray, work that disconnects us from our sources of life rather than moves us toward wholeness.

For work to pray, it must have a sense of vocation attached to it—we must feel some calling toward that work and the wholeness of which it is a part, that there is something holy in good work. "It is by way of the practice of vocation that sanctity and reverence enter the economy," writes Berry, "It was thus possible for traditional cultures to conceive that 'to work is to pray.'"[1] Vocation is a calling and prayer is a call and response, deep calling to deep. For work to pray, to be vocation, it must be brought into a larger conversation. "The idea of vocation attaches to work a cluster of other ideas, including devotion, skill, pride, pleasure, the good stewardship of means and materials," Berry writes.[2] It is these "intangibles of economic value" that keep us from viewing work as "something good only to escape: 'Thank God it's Friday.'"[3]

A "job" or "employment" is the name Berry gives to work that doesn't pray—work that is devoid of affection and only exchanged for money, a kind of prostitution of labor. In Berry's novel *Hannah Coulter,* the title character mourns the loss of her children to such work in a conversation with Andy Catlett. She says:

> One of the attractions of moving away into the life of employment, I think, is being disconnected and free, unbothered by membership. It is a life of beginnings without memories, but it is a life too that ends without being remembered. The life of membership with all its cumbers is traded away for the life of employment that makes itself free by forgetting you clean as a whistle when you are not of any more use. When they get to retirement age, Margaret and Mattie and Caleb will be cast out of place and out of mind like worn-out replaceable parts, to be alone at the last maybe and soon forgotten.
>
> "But the membership," Andy said, "keeps the memories even of horses and mules and milk cows and dogs."[4]

When work is a part of a whole, when it is holy, it is connected to a network of affections and givenness, and so it is held in the memory of the "membership" as Berry calls the community life of his fictional town Port William.

Hannah's worry over her children is that after their long careers, they will retire into a kind of nothingness, their work will not have mattered. In the end, it will be clear that they were only cogs in a mindless wheel. In employment, workers are replaceable; in the membership there is no replacement because work involves the whole of each person, body and soul. Each person leaves his or her mark on the membership and each person is not reducible or replaceable, they are thus held in the memory of the whole—their work endures.

By dividing work from affection, employment in the industrial economy also reinforces the division of the body and the soul or spirit. This is particularly found in the use of technology where the body is often removed, as much as possible, from the work. The body is replaced, instead, by a machine that is meant to join in some communion with the mind, leaving the body as a kind of "dead weight." It also shifts the sources of power, of energy.

• • •

To care well and to work well, we must also be concerned with the question of energy. Work is the use of energy, and tools are our means of harnessing and extending its power through our use. For Berry, there are two sorts of energy. There is biological energy—energy coming from life and returning to it. Such energy is essentially solar powered and when exercised on a properly biological scale it can continue on and on. It is a kind of energy that brings together life. "In an energy economy appropriate to the use of biological energy," writes Berry, "all bodies, plant and animal and human, are joined in a kind of energy community."[5]

This energy is the sort typified by Psalm 104, in which the psalmist proclaims the glory of God and connects the life of the whole creation, including the economics of agriculture to God's own energy and life:

> These all look to you
>> to give them their food in due season;
>> when you give to them, they gather it up;
>>> when you open your hand, they are filled with good things.
>
> When you hide your face, they are dismayed;
>> when you take away their breath, they die
>> and return to their dust.
>
> When you send forth your spirit, they are created;
>> and you renew the face of the ground. (Psalms 104:27–30)

The second kind of energy that concerns Berry is not rooted in life—we access it not through the cycles of return, but through depletion. It is captured only through machines. Such energy is that of oil, gas, and coal—the dead energy of ancient life that can now only be burned up. There is also nuclear energy and other chemical sources, but all of them have in common a remainder of waste rather than return. We can work with these forms of energy only through the medium of machines.

Most often in our time, our work involves a combination of biological and mechanical energy, but when the two meet, the biological almost always becomes subject to the pattern of mechanical energy in some way. In his essay "A Good Scythe," Berry writes about working with a traditional, manual scythe and then a "power scythe" or "weed eater." Berry finds that the "power scythe" brought his work into a kind of pattern that is unnatural and exhausting. "The power scythe, like all motor-driven tools, imposes patterns of endurance that are alien to the body," he writes, "As long as the motor is running there is a pressure to keep going."[6] The problem with the power scythe, and all mechanical energy, is the way it moves us beyond a human scale of work. "As speed increases, care declines," writes Berry, "And so, necessarily, do the skills of responsibility."[7]

The energy of mechanical power unleashed in industrial work is so great that it must be global in order to contain its waste and destruction. No economy that seeks to sustain itself in a particular place could create waste and destruction in the manner of the global economy—it would exhaust both its resources and the livability of its place. A community might be able to survive with a pick-axe-operated coal mine at its center, but an economy that would blast apart the entire mountain and bring in four-story dredging machines would never be able to work within a sustainable community. Indeed, the global economy will eventually exceed even the boundaries of the globe if it doesn't submit to our given, creaturely limits.

● ● ●

Work animated by machine-based energy rather than biological energy is unlikely to enable work rooted in our vocation to serve and keep the creation—it does not bend toward common flourishing. "To argue for a balance between people and their tools, between life and machinery," writes Berry, "is to argue for restraints upon the use of machines."[8] To act within such limits requires humility—a proper understanding of human capacities. It also requires a sense of necessity, the tragic understanding that "much as we long for infinites of power and duration...it is more likely that we will have either to live within our limits, within the human definition, or not live at all."[9]

This conflict in our work, our powers, and our purposes, gets back to the old conflicts of the human condition. Do we work as creatures, limited and yet within the grace and health of the whole, or do we ignore our limits in an effort to follow the old temptation, found in Genesis, to "be as gods" (Genesis 3:5, KJV)?

We know from our history and our religious and cultural inheritances that the path beyond our humanity, our creatureliness, is a path toward damage. Good work on the other hand is a path of healing, a path of wholeness. As Berry writes in his poem "Healing":

Good work finds the way between pride and despair.
It graces with health. It heals with grace.
It preserves the given so that it remains a gift.
By it, we lose loneliness:
we clasp the hands of those who go before us, and the
hands of those who come after us;
we enter the little circle of each other's arms,
and the larger circle of lovers whose hands are joined in
a dance,
and the larger circle of call creatures, passing in and out
of life, who move also in a dance, to a music so subtle and
vast that no ear hears it except in fragments.[10]

The relationship of energy and the tools, of technology and work is also the theme of Berry's famous essay "Why I Am Not Going to Buy a Computer." Written in 1987, at the time when personal computers were still new but were gaining traction, Berry's essay sought to explain why he refused to adopt this new tool. He begins the essay, not directly with the technology, but by stating an obvious relationship that would result from his purchase of a computer: "Like almost everybody else, I am hooked to the energy corporations, which I do not admire."[11] If he were to buy a computer, this purchase would also force him to buy more electricity from the very coal and coal-burning companies that Berry has spent his career writing against. By using this new technology, he would also be taking on new relationships, and in this case, those relationships would be with corporations he does not admire.

Not only this, but the purchase of a computer would disrupt the good relationships he had already established. Wendell Berry writes the manuscripts for his books by hand and then Tanya, his wife, types them out on a manual typewriter. "As she types, she sees things that are wrong and marks them with small checks in the margins," writes Berry. Through this process, Tanya serves as his "best critic" and also a skilled editor because, as Berry writes, "She also understands, sometimes better than I do, what *ought* to be said." The working relationship between Wendell and Tanya Berry results in what Berry calls "a literary cottage industry that works well and pleasantly."[12] To introduce a computer to the mix would solve a problem Berry doesn't have and would possibly disrupt the good relationships that already exist.

Berry's problem isn't with technology per se, but with the ways in which technology changes our relationship with the world and each other. He is not opposed to progress, if it is actually progress, but Berry worries that, "It is as if a whole population has been genetically deprived of the ability to subtract."[13] Technologies are adopted without any thought to the downsides, for ourselves or for the world around us. He refuses to submit humanity or community or the goods of creation to technology—technology is instead judged by these values. In this Berry is similar in his thinking to many Amish communities, whose rejection of many modern technologies is often misunderstood. Rather than rejecting technology outright, each Amish community evaluates new technologies as a community and asks the question of how each new technology will change their work and their relationships.

David Kline, an Amish bishop and friend of Berry's, has described the ways in which different Amish communities have adopted threshing machines. Threshing is a labor-intensive process when performed manually, and yet it is also a means by which neighbors help one another during the wheat harvest. Teams of men go from farm to farm, performing the hard work together while their families prepare big meals with which to end the day. Some Amish communities have decided that they should adopt threshing machines because of the immense labor saving they provide, but others have rejected the machines because for all the time and energy saved, there is a cost in neighborly work and communion. Different communities have answered the question in different ways, but all of them have dealt in some way with the question of subtraction. Those of us thoroughly beholden to the industrial economy have been trained in a kind of math that's all addition. We have difficulty seeing and accounting for the downside of any technology.

There was a striking backlash to "Why I Will Not Buy a Computer" when it was printed in *Harper's Magazine* and the response prompted Berry to write another essay—"Feminism, the Body, and the Machine"—to more fully explore the nature of work and to dismantle the supposed feminism of his critics. Many of his critics said that it was easy for Berry to be rid of a computer because he had a wife, indicating that this was some sort of derogatory or forced collaboration. Berry, giving little credit to his detractors, nonetheless takes up the task of exploring the nature of work and the ways in which contemporary assumptions about work serve to degrade the labor of both sexes.

Central to his task is the destruction of the boundaries between home and work. For Berry, the most important economy is always the household economy, and its aim is subsistence, or the sustenance of the household in its place. Work is then the proper use and care that maintains the household toward its flourishing. The problem of our contemporary lives is that we have separated household from economy. The world of work outside of the household has become the place where we are productive, whereas the household itself is consumptive.

Divorce is then the operative paradigm—divorce of economy and household results in the functional divorce of the couple. "Marriage" writes Berry, "has now taken the form of divorce: a prolonged and impassioned negotiation as to how things shall be divided."[14] During the course of such a marriage the "couple will typically consume a large quantity of merchandise and a large portion of each other."[15]

Division and separation are at the heart of the industrial economy, so it is no wonder that divorce would be its form. The industrial economy has divided the labor of men from women, the work of children from their families, the work of families from their households and communities. And what has resulted ultimately is a division of the self—a result that can be seen in the tragic scandals of our economy in which the personal virtue of a person has been left behind at the office door.

That this economy of division now includes women in its ranks is no improvement in Berry's eyes. "How," he asks, "can women improve themselves by submitting to the same specialization, degradation, trivialization and tyrannization of work that men have submitted to?"[16] The answer is not an equality of pay, but a liberation of both men and women from the life of "employment."

Instead of the model in which two parents work outside the home to pay for professional childcare services, takeout food, and expensive means of entertainment and exercise for their tired minds and bodies, Berry proposes a more holistic vision of work where the couple "makes around itself a household economy that involves the work of both wife and husband, that gives them a measure of economic independence and self-protection, a measure of self-employment, a measure of freedom, as well as a common ground and a common satisfaction."[17]

This ideal of work may be hard for many to swallow, even if they are sympathetic to the vision. One must understand here, as elsewhere, that Berry's work is often aimed at revealing the ways that our economy prevents people from living as they should. "My interest is not to quarrel with individuals, men or women, who work away from home," he writes, "but rather to ask why we should consider this general working away from home to be a desirable state of things, either for people or for marriage, for our society or for our country."[18]

That said, "Feminism, the Body, and the Machine" is an essay that has haunted my own mind and life for many years and one whose goods I have tried to live out as best I can within my own household economy. As I've discovered in my own life and work, Berry's vision does provide livable possibilities for those now bound to nine-to-five, forty-hour-a-week jobs performed in cubicles—it provides a direction in which we can move toward better work even if it cannot be fully embraced. The first key in this move is to seek greater simplicity in our life and a change of our desires. In order for our work to join in a more coherent household economy we must readjust our vision, asking not how much we can have but how little can we live on? How frugally can we live? Those questions are not aimed at deprivation, but at a livable standard. This means that many expensive technologies and toys must be set aside—a cable bill or car payment or the maintenance and insurance for two cars, for instance, should not be taken for granted as simply parts of adult life. To be freed from relentless work is made possible by lowering our standards of living.

Another key is to think about our households as places of production rather than consumption. This is a common point in Berry's work, but he means much more by it than having something to sell at the farmers market or turning out quilts in our spare time. Instead, we should understand that when we make a meal at home, rather than picking up takeout, we are making a move toward a productive rather than consumptive household. When we grow some of the ingredients for that meal we take a step further. The more we can do for ourselves, the more we are making the switch in our household from a center of consumption to production. And this goes for such things as childcare, as well.

This last point brings us to the important idea of "free labor." Much of our confusion about work stems, in Berry's view, from our incessant attachment to a paycheck. Such an attachment denies the idea of work as a gift. Reflecting on the critics who were upset to find that Tanya Berry types Wendell's manuscripts, he writes, "What appears to infuriate them most is their supposition that she works for nothing. They assume—and this is the orthodox assumption of the industrial economy—that the only help worth giving is not given at all, but sold. Love, friendship, neighborliness, compassion, duty—what are they? We are realists. We will be most happy to receive your check."[19]

* * *

When we exist in a world of gift, in which we ourselves are given, then our own labors must be gifts to those around us. To refuse that possibility is to refuse the thanksgiving to which we are properly called. Or, to put it another way, if we are not willing to see our lives and the creation as gifts, then we are not able to properly acknowledge our debts. Being so free, we then feel as though it is in our right to say that others owe us. Thus we can easily *sell* our labors, without any sense of obligation that perhaps we really *owe* them. That some should give their labors freely is then, properly, the response of those who owe what cannot be repaid—which includes us all.

There is a sense of this in the Lord's Prayer, in which we pray that we will be forgiven what we owe, just as we forgive those who owe us. There is acknowledgment, from the start, that we are in debt to God and that we are in some ways in debt to one another. This is far more than the wrongs or trespasses of sin, but rather a proper understanding of our relationships—God has given us what we cannot repay and we cannot expect others to repay us for what we have given them. It all exists in an economy of gifts that stand outside any possibility of exchange.

To recognize our common participation in the giving of our gifts through labor leads to thanksgiving and also a kind of respect for labor. Gandhi, after reading the English Christian writer John Ruskin, came to respect labor to such a degree that he used a pencil down to its very nib as a way of honoring the human work that had gone into making it. Such respect is a kind of thanksgiving for the common gift of work. It seems fitting then to end this chapter with a short reflection on Berry's understanding of thanksgiving—the proper response for any given creature to its giver. In a way thanksgiving is at the heart of all of Berry's work on givenness, but it only occasionally surfaces explicitly.

For Berry, thanksgiving is fully living into our givenness—it is the acceptance that our life is a miracle. To be thankful is to take pleasure in our existence and in the things that make that existence possible. "In this pleasure," writes Berry, "we experience and celebrate our dependence and our gratitude, for we are living from mystery, from creatures we did not make and powers we cannot comprehend."[20] Berry is here speaking particularly of the pleasure that comes in our eating and its attendant thanksgiving, but he is also necessarily speaking of the pleasure of membership. Our lives are indebted to other lives and dependent upon them. Each life taken on its own might look like a negative balance, but together, within the context of the membership, these debts are cancelled into a whole in which fore-giving and thanks-giving play an integral role.

Through this gratitude and proper understanding of indebtedness, we are able to gain the freedom to become more generous ourselves. Reflecting on this, Berry writes in *The Sabbath Poems, "I"* (1993):

> You have become a sort of grave
> containing much that was
> and is no more in time, beloved
> then, now, and always...
> Now more than ever you can be
> generous toward each day
> that comes, young, to disappear...
> Every day you have less reason
> not to give yourself away.[21]

Those last lines get at the core of the ethics of givenness. When we come to truly understand our givenness, which is also our indebtedness and embeddedness in the whole of the creation, then our response must be to give as we have been given, even fore-give as we have been fore-given. All pretenses that attend the accomplishments of our own work, all illusions of making value or owning something, is but a debt unaccounted, a gift accepted without thanks. If we want to embrace Berry's insights our first and most profound response should be to fill our days with thanksgiving. It is in that practice that we will finally begin to recover who we are and what we should be about in this world, this creation, this gift.

CHAPTER SIX

Sabbath

•••••••••••••••••

DELIGHT AND THE REORIENTATION OF DESIRE

The sun is beginning its tilt toward the west as cicadas buzz and summer tanagers click from the white and green branches of black hickory. We follow the trail up, over the jackfork formations of shale and sandstone, a slow climb along ridgelines. My youngest daughter, not yet two, runs up and down the trail, doubling her steps and stopping only to pick up a hickory nut or investigate an odd leaf. My oldest daughter, four, skips and bounds along, swinging an Easter basket repurposed for berries.

We come to a stop, just as the summer sweat is beginning to break on our skin. In a clearing cut for power lines, now over-grown with weeds and shrubs, are thorny blackberry bushes hung with red and purple fruit like skinny two toned Christmas trees. We begin foraging, our hands moving with care, dropping berries in the basket and in our mouths in equal measure. Our youngest, stationing herself strategically by the basket, eats the most, her lips turning crimson.

No one planted these berries. They came from birds being birds, soil being soil, sun being sun. We could pick our fill and there would be more, not only the sweet purple berries but red ones that will ripen in another week, green ones that will ripen in another month—the supply will be continuous over the summer. Our interest is not in filling any basket—it is simply to have a snack, to collect free food, to enjoy an hour away from any machines or screens or work. This is a moment of Sabbath—it is a time of rest in the abundance of creation.

If we are to recover what it means to be a creature, to live a given life in a given world, then Sabbath will be a central practice. It is in Sabbath that we learn to rest and wrest ourselves from the anxieties of achievement, of making and doing, that clamor inside and out.

"It invites us to rest," writes Berry. "It asks us to notice that while we rest the world continues without our help. It invites us to find delight in the world's beauty and abundance."[1] In our greed that rushes to consume the world to our own destruction, "it may be asking us also to consider that if we choose not to honor it and care well for it, the world will continue in our absence."[2]

Sabbath has not only been a central idea and principle for Berry—it has been a regular and anchoring practice. For six days a week, Berry works and as anyone who has had the fortune to visit him knows, he is loath to break the pattern of those days. On Sundays, however, Berry rests from his labor, takes a walk in the woods, and sometimes goes to church, where his wife plays the piano. It is on Sunday afternoons that visitors are welcomed on occasion, hosted on the porch or his living room lit only by the sunlight pouring in. It is on these Sundays that Berry has been engaged for several decades in one of his central poetic projects—Sabbath poems. The subject matter of these poems ranges widely, from the delights of creation to sadness and lament. But in all of them, there is a quality of the rest from which they are born, the silence they have broken and to which they return.

On his Sabbath walks in the woods, Berry writes: "I experience a lovely freedom from expectations—other people's and also my own. I go free from the tasks and intentions of my workdays, and so my mind becomes hospitable to unintended thoughts: to what I am very willing to call inspiration."[3] The poems that come are not, then, the work of a poet trying to force a line, but rather a gift received from the given world. "If the Muse leaves me alone," writes Berry, "I leave her alone. To be quiet, even wordless, in a good place is a better gift than poetry."[4]

It is in these poems that Berry is able to grasp what is ultimately at the base of all good work. It is all, though not without effort, rooted in gift—"Where we arrive by work, we stay by grace."[5] Though a garden should be cultivated, its soil tended and sowed toward flourishing, weeded and protected from pests, its ultimate produce is based in the gift of the abundant creation. The Sabbath is a time when we are reminded of this; accepting the manna that cannot be hoarded, picking blackberries that provide delight without cultivation.

It is in the same way that we are reminded of the truth of the creation—that our work, though called and needed, is not necessary. The world will continue without us and came long before us. Our work is to live from and with these gifts so that we can use what time we have, what little time we have, to tend their flourishing rather than exploit them for the gains that will soon fade with the rot.

The practice of Sabbath also has the effect of elevating the value of labor and of the people engaged in it. It is not a break so that we might become renewed and refreshed for more work, but is rather a time when we live in the simple reality that we are creatures whose lives are given by God. On the Sabbath, we are able to *be* apart from our achievements.

• • •

Berry writes that Sabbath rest is needed, in part, "in order to understand that the providence or the productivity of the living world, the most essential work, continues while we rest."[6] This continuing work, in which we must live in acceptance and delight, is "far more complex and wonderful than any work we have ever done or will ever do. It is far more complex and wonderful than we will ever understand."[7] It is this work, the dynamic energy humming through the creation, that is the measure of our own work. To violate it is to violate our place and our membership within it; it is to live against the standard of our given selves. To practice Sabbath is a means of learning this measure; to violate the Sabbath is to transgress our standard as human beings.

"From the biblical point of view, the earth and our earthly livelihood are conditional gifts," writes Berry. "We may possess the land given to us, that we are given to, only by remembering our intimate kinship to it."[8] Sabbath is a way in which we can begin this remembering. We stop so that we can learn again that we live not by the bread we have earned, but from the sustaining breath of God that we share in the great exchange of all being.

This remembering is aided by taking it outdoors. Like the Seventh Day Adventists, who encourage their members to take nature walks on their Sabbath day, Berry believes that Sabbath is a practice best performed in the open creation. "The idea of the Sabbath gains in meaning as it is brought out-of-doors and into a place where nature's principles of self-sustaining wholeness and health are still evident," writes Berry. It is here that "the natural and the supernatural, the heavenly and the earthly, the soul and the body, the wondrous and the ordinary, all appear to occur together in one fabric of creation."[9]

In the Sabbath, the creation is complete, it is whole, it is finished. This is an old idea, one that refigures the idea of that first Sabbath rest not as a time when God ceased from creation, but as a day in which God crowns all things with delight. The deep harmony and peace of all creation is, in this interpretation, God's final creative act.

The medieval rabbi Rashi claimed that the Sabbath was the day in which God did not cease from creation, but rather made *menuha,* which is God's restful delight in the creation. As Norman Wirzba writes in his book *Living the Sabbath,* "*Menuha,* not humanity, completes creation. God's rest or *shabbat,* especially when understood within a *menuha* context, is not simply a cessation from activity but rather the lifting up and celebration of everything."[10] So it is that Sabbath is not a time in which we escape from the "everyday" but rather realize the reality of the creation that is beneath it. This is a truth that we embrace on the Sabbath but find glimmers of elsewhere in our everyday lives.

Christians have often been poor at practicing the Sabbath, imagining it to be a Jewish practice for which Jesus showed apparent disregard. But a careful reading of the Gospels shows a very different reality. Jesus's work was not to diminish the Sabbath but to extend it, welcoming all into its embrace. He came to proclaim a new age of Sabbath, an epoch of jubilee in which the division between heaven and earth would join in the great, "one fabric of creation."

So it is that the Sabbath, if practiced well, is no refuge from our everyday lives, but a reorientation that should come to permeate them. Our work, if done well, will become more and more continuous with the rest of Sabbath. One hopes that most of us have had a hint of this experience; a time in our lives when our work and pleasure were the same, when our labor and our rest were united.

Berry, as we've noted, shows disdain for the kinds of work that look forward to an escape—"Thank God it's Friday." Such work has no Sabbath in it and so it also has none of the continuous fabric of creation. Such work can be, and most certainly is, damaging to the creation. Instead, work guided and living in the presence of the Sabbath uses this day of delight as every day's pattern and standard. Rather than seeing how endlessly productive we can be, we learn to wait and see what we can allow the creation to do on its own.

One of the writers who has influenced Berry, the Japanese agriculturalist Masanobu Fukuoka, pioneered a philosophy of agriculture called "do-nothing farming." Of course, this farming takes some doing, but it starts with asking not how much we can do, but how little we can get away with. Instead of actively composting, for instance, Fukuoka advocated directly mixing manure and stubble matter on the fields and letting nature do the rest. This is the way of Sabbath.

Sabbath is a way by which our work is liberated and reminded of its place and purpose. Abraham Joshua Heschel, wrote in his now classic book *The Sabbath: Its Meaning for Modern Man*:

> He who wants to enter the holiness of the day must first lay down the profanity of clattering commerce, of being yoked to toil. He must go away from the screech of dissonant days, from the nervousness and fury of acquisitiveness and the betrayal in embezzling his own life. He must say farewell to manual work and learn to understand that the world has already been created and will survive without the help of man.[11]

The Sabbath is a discipline by which we learn to live in the abundance of creation. It is a gift that requires no work but the task of acceptance. As Berry writes in one of his Sabbath poems:

> Six days of work are spent
> To make a Sunday quiet
> That Sabbath may return.
> It comes in unconcern;
> We cannot earn or buy it.[12]

This makes Sabbath something different from vacation—a concept that is marked, even in its etymology, by absence rather than presence. The idea of vacation is simply another part of the industrial economy that moves us, even while we seek to rest. "To rest, we are persuaded, we must 'get away,'" writes Berry, "But getting away involves us in the haste, speed, and noise, the auxiliary pandemonium of escape."[13] Sabbath is meant not to help us leave the workaday world, but to return to the world, to be present to those places we have forgotten in our frenzied movement. As Berry expresses it:

There is a day
when the road neither
comes nor goes, and the way
is not a way but a place.[14]

Sabbath brings us to that place. It is the road by which we stay.

Practically, a helpful rule for anyone who seeks to practice the Sabbath as Berry suggests, would be to adopt something like the traditional Jewish probation against travel on the Sabbath. I once lived in a neighborhood near a Hasidic community. I would rarely see members of the community except on Saturdays, when the prohibition against using cars would mean that Hasids were walking about in visits to friends or on their way to the synagogue.

While my own family doesn't entirely follow the prohibition against traveling in automobiles on the day we practice Sabbath, we do try to limit our travel and stick to a small radius. The rules are not laws, but it is helpful to find some limit that will help protect your practice of Sabbath from the constant draw toward activity and movement. Even the wild can be consumed, as any visitor to a major national park is well aware. Create the limits that will allow the Sabbath be a time of accepting the abundance of creation rather than its consumption.

• • •

In the biblical idea of Sabbath there are several cycles, weekly and annual. Every seven years, the Jewish people were to leave their fields fallow. This was a time to give the land a rest and to let a kind of re-wilding take place. The practice had the function not only of helping rebuild soil fertility, but also of reminding the people of the creation's abundance, it's flourishing apart from human activity. Berry sees this kind of practice continued in the leaving of wild places, areas untouched by the ambitions of production. He writes: "The farm must yield a place to the forest, not as a wood lot, or even as a necessary agricultural principle, but as a sacred grove—a place where the Creation is let alone, to serve as instruction, example, refuge; a place for people to go, free of work and presumption, to let themselves alone."[15]

There is also a time, in the Jewish ideal of Sabbath, when every seven cycles of Sabbath years (roughly every forty-nine years) prisoners were to be set free and the land reverted to its original owners. This was a means to correct against the concentration of wealth and debts. These were called years of Jubilee and as we have noted, much of Jesus's actions and teachings around Sabbath were aimed at ushering in a new age of Jubilee. When Jesus heals those who have been excluded from the community through their disease, he is drawing them back into the whole; he is not diminishing the aim of the Sabbath but fulfilling it.

The Sabbath is then a time in which we are able to find freedom. It is rooted in the Exodus experience in which the people of Israel were liberated from the relentless demand to make bricks in Egypt without rest. In Egypt the limits of nature and human work were without limit in an economy whose masters pretended to be divine. The Sabbath was to usher in an alternative, a time in which we "accept Nature's limits and our own." It is when we arrive at our limit that, as Berry says, "we must be still."[16] To practice Sabbath is a means of resisting the culture of commodity that invites us to go beyond the bounds of the human. As Old Testament scholar Walter Brueggemann writes, "The Sabbath rest of God is the acknowledgement that God and God's people in the world are not commodities to be dispatched for endless production.... Rather they are subjects situated in an economy of neighborliness."[17]

This neighborliness is a Sabbath economy in which our whole social order is questioned and reoriented. By entering into Sabbath, we break with the noise of the world, and become attuned to a truth beyond the pretenders to our meaning. In his poem "III:2007" Berry invites the reader to pray for the scientists, CEOs, and other elites of the industrial economy:

...that they too
may wake to a day without hope
that in their smallness they
may know the greatness of Earth
and Heaven by which they so far
live....[18]

This is a prayer for truth but also for a re-visioning of the social order. When Moses went to Pharaoh, asking for permission to go to the desert and celebrate the Sabbath, the great king had the chance for such reorientation, but in refusing the truth he accepted the tragic result—plague and death and loss. So it will be with our "pharaoh's" if they do not learn the "greatness of Earth / and Heaven by which they so far / live."

In Sabbath, our imaginations are sparked so that we can look past the urgent call of the day's needs and the day's news to see the wholeness of the creation. Sabbath is not simply rest, but a revolutionary act in which we begin to live into a new social reality. As Walter Brueggemann writes, "Sabbath...is an occasion for reimagining all of social life away from coercion and competition to compassionate solidarity. Such solidarity is imaginable and capable of performance only when the driven-ness of acquisitiveness is broken.... Sabbath is an invitation to receptivity, an acknowledgement that what is needed is given and need not be seized."[19] This idea of common gift, acknowledged and accepted rather than seized, is key to our recovery of the creaturely life.

Like so much of Berry's writing and ideas, it is easy to be captured by the vision but frustrated when we look at our own lives and imagine how we might practice it. How do we find the retreat into this Sabbath world where we can be reoriented while living in a place with busy streets and our only options for wilderness are parks that hardly embody the creation in its abundant autonomy? The answer is that we must engage our imaginations and learn to translate these truths, as all truths must be translated, to our own places and contexts. Even city sidewalks host feral grasses that break through, a wild whisper that signals what will come when the city's noise finally fades. Sabbath is a reality that can break through anywhere if we learn to have the eyes to see it.

There are some efforts underway that might help us enter into the Sabbath life wherever we live. In New York City, there is a group called "Sabbath Manifesto" that is seeking to renew the practice of Sabbath for millennial urbanites and others of us who have lost the meaning and practice of Sabbath. Through campaigns like the "National Day of Unplugging" and such merchandise as cell phone sleeping bags, they invite a people addicted to the constant hum of activity to free a day from all the noise. Their "Ten Principles" offer open guidance that makes for a meaningful Sabbath in the modern world, including advice such as "avoid technology," "get outside," and "connect with loved ones."[20] They even have an app.

Though presented in a different context and form than Berry's own call for Sabbath, "Sabbath Manifesto" is drawing on the same scriptures and traditions for the same end. If we can take one day to live apart from the world that always answers our manipulations, a day without focusing on being productive or consumptive, then we can begin to live more and more into the abundant creation. And with time, the anxieties that fuel so much of modern life will fade so that we can tune our lives again to the gracious life offered us all.

CHAPTER SEVEN

Stability

BECOMING NATIVE IN AN AGE OF EVERYWHERE

In Wallace Stegner's novel *Angle of Repose*, a character ponders the possibility of home in modern America:

> I wonder if ever again Americans can have that experience of returning to a home place so intimately known, profoundly felt, deeply loved, and absolutely submitted to? It is not quite true that you can't go home again. I have done it, coming back here. But it gets less likely. We have had too many divorces, we have consumed too much transportation, we have lived too shallowly in too many places.[1]

This insight from one of Berry's most important teachers names a problem at the heart of many others. We live mobile lives in a global economy and so we find roots hard to put down, and yet we need them, for our health and the health of the places of which we are a part. Like plants transplanted too often, our lives and the lives of our communities wither rather than flourish, momentarily propped up by chemical fertilizers that cannot sustain us over the long run.

Our problem is contemporary in character, but not in kind. There seems to be something in the human condition that is restless unless formed in stability. Perhaps it is an aspect of our aversion to creatureliness, our desire to live without context in a freedom defined by being unbound and unlimited. The old masters of the spiritual life saw this as a temptation of the devil.

There is a story from *The Sayings of the Desert Fathers* that makes this point. A seeker troubled by restlessness once visited Abba Arsenius. "My thoughts trouble me, saying, 'You can neither fast nor work; at least go and visit the sick, for that is also charity,'" the seeker said. The old monk recognized the suggestion of demons and so said to him, "Go, eat, drink, sleep, do no work, only do not leave your cell." He said this, according to the *Sayings*, "For he knew that steadfastness in the cell keeps a monk in the right way."[2]

This problem of restlessness is what drew St. Benedict to make stability one of the central vows of his communities. He understood that like the stability of marriage, stability of place and community help us gain the necessary endurance for real growth to occur, enough time for our roots to grow strong enough to push through the rocks and clay. It is this same restlessness that makes belonging to a place a central theme in Wendell Berry's work. It is a case Berry articulated most forcefully in his manifesto of the agrarian life, *The Unsettling of America*.

In *The Unsettling of America*, Berry begins with an indictment that he admits is "too simply put" and yet clearly names the problem at the heart of our lives and economy:

> One of the peculiarities of the white race's presence in
> America is how little attention has been applied to it. As

a people, wherever we have been, we have never really intended to be. The continent was said to have been discovered by an Italian who was on his way to India.... Once the unknown of geography was mapped, the industrial marketplace became the new frontier, and we continued, with largely the same motives and with increasing haste and anxiety, to displace ourselves—no longer with unity of direction, like a migrant flock, but like the refugees from a broken anthill. In our own time we have invaded foreign lands and the moon with the high-toned patriotism of the conquistadors, and with the same mixture of fantasy and avarice.[3]

Those who have not followed this impulse have invariably been its victims, overtaken by the exploiters. But ultimately even the winners in this economy, those "unconscious of the effects of [their] life or livelihood," will become its victims. We all must, despite our best efforts, live somewhere and the earth is our only viable option for a healthy and flourishing future. "Even the richest and most mobile," writes Berry, "will soon find it hard to escape the noxious effluents and fumes of their various public services."[4]

In an effort to escape the ties and limits of place, then, we have initiated the destruction of *every* place. This is a reality starkly realized in the crisis of our climate, which is inescapable, though the most vulnerable still suffer its most dire consequences; conqueror and victim eventually become one. "In order to understand our own time and predicament and the work that is to be done," Berry thus suggests, "we would do well to shift the terms and say that we are divided between exploitation and nurture." This is a division that is "not only between persons but within persons."[5]

As products of a culture and economy rife with exploitation, we must all see that the tendency toward exploitation is embedded within us, a cultured second nature. But we are not entirely lost to our exploitation. As human beings, some remnant of the ancient wisdom of rooting and staying and nurture remain in our traditions. The work for us now is to cultivate this cultivating side and to quiet the clamor of conquest. The challenge and its solutions are both spiritual, rooted in the deepest parts of our desires and heart. As Berry writes:

> It seems to me that our people are suffering terribly from a sort of spiritual nomadism a loss of meaningful contact with the earth and the earth's cycles of birth, growth and death. They lack the vital morality and spirituality that can come only from such contact: the sense, for instance, of their dependence on the earth, and the sense of eternal mystery surrounding life on earth, which is its ultimate and most disciplining context.[6]

The task of recovery is to renew that contact with the earth's cycles, to recover the sense of "eternal mystery surrounding life on earth" by deepening our relationship with our places.

● ● ●

Our relationship with a place is formed by our desires for it. "The exploiters' goal is money, profit," writes Berry. The exploiter sees in each place the profit that can be had from it and when that profit is gone, the exploiter leaves whether it is for a place with more resources or a place with a better job. "[T]he nurturer's goal is health—his land's health, his own, his family's, his community's, his country's." In these goals there is a wholeness of people and place; there is recognition that, "Neither nature nor people alone can produce human sustenance, but only the two together, culturally wedded."[7] So it is that we need culture and agriculture together in order to have places and communities of nurture.

To see an example of such nurture at work in opposition to exploitation we should look at Berry's collaboration with the photographer Ralph Meatyard in defense of the Red River Gorge. This gorge, in east central Kentucky, is a place of profound natural beauty and ecological diversity; a place where the beauty of creation bursts forth.

The U.S. Army Corps of Engineers, however, saw the gorge as a good sight for a dam and recreation lake. Berry and his friend Ralph Meatyard, known for his portraits of Thomas Merton, created a book together as a kind of argument for the place, an invitation toward its nurture rather than its destruction. There, Berry wrote that "the world cannot be discovered by a journey of miles, no matter how long, but only by a spiritual journey, a journey of one inch, very arduous and humbling and joyful, by which we arrive at the ground at our feet, and learn to be at home."[8] This homecoming requires us to stay long enough to move beyond the surface. It means that we must look down to recognize the beauty *here*, rather than clearing the trees so that we can turn our gaze toward the horizon. It means that we must adapt to our landscapes rather than simply adapting them to our desires.

To take the spiritual journey of discovering our place we must escape the thinking that the world is small. Such an idea is available only to those who would reduce the world, leaving a great deal out. "The life of this world is small to those who think it is," writes Berry, "and the desire to enlarge it makes it smaller, and can reduce it finally to nothing."[9] So went the mind of the Corps of Engineers who saw the Red River Gorge as a small place that needed enlarging and improvement; so go the many "developments" that destroy small places in the name of jobs and growth and progress.

The call to remain in a place, to be stable within it, is a call to live into the proper scale of human life and action. As the writer and new monasticism leader Jonathan Wilson-Hartgrove writes, "I am convinced that we lose something essential to our existence as creatures if we do not recognize our fundamental need for stability."[10] To find a place, to "stop somewhere" as Berry's friend Gary Snyder puts it, is to lay out the border for our growth, the proper limits in which we can find health and exercise care. "The reality that is responsibly manageable by human intelligence," Berry writes, "is much nearer in scale to a small rural community or urban neighborhood than to the 'globe.'"[11] We can save the Red River Gorge, but not the world. Our hope comes from the many people rooted in and devoted to the care and health of their particular places. We must escape the myth of being at home in the whole of the world.

In his book *Consilience*, E.O. Wilson writes, "Today the entire planet has become home ground."[12] Berry responds to this claim writing, "No human has ever known, let along imagined, the entire planet…. But if we are to know any part of planet intimately, particularly, precisely, and with affection, then we must live somewhere in particular for a long time."[13]

Though it might seem contradictory, this deep rootedness in a particular place is essential in the face of such a truly global challenge as climate change. In her critical book on the subject, *This Changes Everything*, Naomi Klein lays out the challenges facing the planet and its people. But the hope she finds isn't in the major centers of power, the engines of technological progress, or large-scale legislation. She sees the work of fighting climate change beginning in the many placed communities around the world that are working to save what they love. "The power of this ferocious love," writes Klein, "is what the resource companies and their advocates in government inevitably underestimate, precisely because no amount of money can extinguish it. When what is being fought for is an identity, a culture, a beloved place that people are determined to pass on to their grandchildren...there is nothing companies can offer as a bargaining chip."[14] It is the cultivation and recovery of such a love of place that is among our greatest hopes.

The difficulty in our time is that just as we seem to have lost the art of marriage, we have also lost the art of loving our places. We must be present to our places and to one another in order to begin the work of love and care. But our society has made the manufactured spaces of consumer society our anchors, the habitats for our living. One trained in the habits and patterns of Starbucks can find comfort in virtually any store, small differences aside. They will always have the same drink of choice, the same wi-fi connection, familiar furniture, and consistent color tones. One could list a host of other commercial spaces that offer the same comforts.

Our lives online expand this problem even more. We have manipulated our experience of space to such a degree that when we are before a screen we can be "virtually here" while being virtually anywhere. This truth is extended through new technologies such as "enhanced reality" glasses that enable us to conform our vision closer to our own desires and "virtual reality" technologies that are increasingly enclosing the experience of the senses within an easily malleable technological space. While the first period of industrialization centered on changing our environment to meet our needs, our present age completes our control by enclosing our experience of the world into a synthetic, malleable reality.

In order to move against this, we must follow the advice of the Senegalese environmentalist Baba Dioum, who advises that "we will conserve only what we love, we will love only what we understand, and we will understand only what we are taught." We must therefore develop a curriculum for being where we are so that we can know, understand, and love our places. We must develop this curriculum so that we can ultimately be a part of their flourishing, care, and resurrection.

In his essay "Going to Work," Berry offers a "curriculum of questions" intended to guide us in the work we need to begin and continue. Among these questions is a series of elaborations of the question *"Where are we?"*:

> What is the place in which we are preparing to do our work? What happened here in geologic time? What is the nature, what is the *genius*, of this place? What, if we weren't here, would nature be doing here? What will the nature of the place permit us to do here without exhausting either the place itself or the birthright of those who will come later? What, even, might nature help us do

here? Under what conditions, imposed by the genius of the place and the genius of our own arts, might our work here be healthful and beautiful?[15]

In answering these questions, we will be well on our way toward developing the knowledge and understanding necessary for affection to take root; we will begin the process Berry's friend the geneticist and plant breeder Wes Jackson has called "becoming native."

Berry's defense of farmers and farmland and the rural communities they are a part of does not mean that he believes everyone should farm or that all should live in rural places. However, Berry does believe that there is something in farming done well that helps one become native and enables one to ask and answer the necessary questions of a place. Those of us who are not farmers, then, should learn to talk with good farmers as our teachers in the realities of our place. We should also try our best to grow something of our own in order to learn what we can of where we are, a kind of necessary exercise in place discovery. Is your soil acidic or basic? Does it tend toward clay or sandy loam? What is the organic content and what does that tell you about the past treatment of this place? These are things that can be discovered through the process of growing something for yourself from your local soils.

"To live as a farmer," writes Berry, "one has to come into the local watershed and local ecosystem, and deal well or poorly with them.... If one wishes to farm well, and agrarianism inclines to that wish above all, then one must submit to the unending effort to change one's mind and ways to fit one's farm."[16] This agrarian standard should become the standard of all our work, whatever it is. If we are to be a placed people, living stable lives toward health and care, we should work to change our minds and ways to fit our local ecosystems and watersheds. This is work that will require our creativity, imagination, and intelligence in a way that our minds, accustomed and adapted to the responsive reality of screens, are not well trained. In order to engage in this work, we must then acquire new habits that enable us to be present and local and neighborly.

In his essay "Where Have All the Joiners Gone," Bill McKibben offers a stark picture of the challenge before us: "A meteorite could fall on your cul-de-sac tomorrow, disappearing your neighbors, and the routines of your daily life wouldn't change."[17] The challenge for us is to embed and entangle ourselves in one another's lives and the life of our places so that both our neighborhoods and neighbors matter. A good question to begin would be to ask how we might make our neighbors more indispensable? How can we make our places more integral to our conscious lives?

Following Berry, many have begun this work by disentangling themselves from the economy of nowhere to become a part of the economy of somewhere. A local food economy is a good place to start, making the farmers market our primary rather than secondary source of food. When we do this, we can begin to learn the situation of our places and care about the fate of the farmers who raise the pigs for our breakfast bacon or the greens for our salads. Rather than making such food an exchangeable option, we should experiment with commitment to our local economies to the degree that we would go without if these farmers were not in business. Their lives would then be entwined with ours, their sacrifice our sacrifice, their pain our pain.

This is the idea behind Community Supported Agriculture programs in which customers buy "shares" in the produce of a farm. In the best scenario customer and farmer experience the same devastation from a sudden flood or benefit from seasonable rains. Though this is often more ideal than reality, the best CSAs do enable farmers and customers to share in risks and rewards.

Another answer is to return to economies of sharing. Rural communities once hosted organizations called "granges" that served as a storehouse for shared tools and resources. In its contemporary arrangement, a group of neighbors could agree to share a tiller and lawn mower among themselves since no one person needs such equipment all the time. These neighbors could also buy loads of compost or mulch collectively, thus cutting the costs. Churches have a real opportunity to organize these groups in their neighborhoods and serve as pick up and drop off places for the grange.

Though it uses the tools of the Internet, which would have little appeal to Berry, Acts of Sharing (actsofsharing.com) is a social application that is animated by a similar impulse of place making and community building. Through an online tool that allows members to list the possessions they are willing to share in common with others, communities such as churches or neighborhoods can create local sharing economies. Need a chainsaw for a temporary project? Acts of Sharing allows you to see that Jane in your church has one to share. In their partnership with Common Change, this organization also enables communities to pool resources to help the people and projects they care about out of their common financial resources.

A recovery of the parish model of church could also be a helpful return to our places. Though one's choice of place to worship can be guided by a number of important concerns, there is no doubt that where we worship is deeply formed by the practices of consumerist society. What if we dedicated ourselves to life within the boundaries of our parish churches, kept to the local zip code, or even began to discover and live within our church's watershed?

There is a movement beginning called "watershed discipleship" which seeks to help Christians reimagine their lives within their ecological rather than political boundaries. Pioneered by Ched Myers, this movement asks us to begin to see what it means to be a disciple of Christ within our watersheds, a naturally defined ecological region. Like Berry's curriculum of questions, it begins with asking *where are we?* If I were to say Little Rock, Arkansas, I would be naming both a region defined by the Osage Indians and then codified by colonial surveyors. To say Little Rock is to name the town designated first by French explorers. Now it is a place with city limits and municipal services. To say Little Rock is to speak of a social and political space whose geography is subject to those boundaries.

If instead I say that I live in the Maumelle River Watershed, I am naming a geological and ecological reality. When it rains, the water that runs from my roof runs into a creek that runs eventually into the Maumelle River and then to the Arkansas River and then to the Mississippi River and then to the Gulf of Mexico. By seeing my place defined by where the water flows,

I am brought into a kind of ecological commons with those whose water also flows here. Since both humans and creatures are dependent upon this water for the health of our lives, we must take an interest in its care. If I ask, how can I best be a creature *here*, how can I be a disciple of Christ *here*, this geological and ecological boundary is more helpful for my understanding than the political and historic boundaries of this place, though they too should inform my presence within it.

This work of finding our place and becoming a part of it is not easy, nor does it have an end. As Berry writes of defining his farming by its place, being a neighbor in a neighborhood, "is a hard education which lasts all one's life, never to be completed, and it almost certainly will involve mistakes."[18] It is work that begins with stopping, seeking to find a place to which we can belong, and becoming its member. It is to this work of membership that we turn next.

CHAPTER EIGHT

Membership

JOINING THE COMMUNITY OF CREATION

When the apostle Paul, frustrated by a contentious and divided Corinthian church, attempted to describe the unity the church should embody he turned to the language of membership: "For just as the body is one and has many members, and all the members of the body, though many, are one body, so it is with Christ" (1 Corinthians 12:12). It is in this idea of membership that the apostle was able to acknowledge difference and variety while at the same time maintaining unity. This unity is made not through the purity of identity, but in a kind of coherent relationality, a wholeness. It is in such a membership that our lives are made complete by being brought into communion with others.

Wendell Berry, likewise, uses the language of membership to describe the wholeness that is embodied in a place. Rather than the term "resident," which seems too passive, simply holding ground, or "citizen," which is dependent on political identity, "membership" is a term that can include the whole of a place—its people, but also its animals and land, its history and future, its town and country. Membership is the name for the belonging we are a part of in the creation. It is in the membership that health and disease are held in common; where, as St. Paul puts it, "if one member suffers, all suffer together with it; if one member is honored, all rejoice together with it" (1 Corinthians 12:26).

The membership is a reality in which our fates are in common because our life is in common. To save one part, we must save all. As Berry writes, "If we want to save the land, we must save the people who belong to the land. If we want to save the people, we must save the land the people belong to."[1] Our lives are entangled and bound up with each other—people and land and other creatures—so that they can only find their flourishing when the whole flourishes together. In fact, this connection of all things is at our very essence as creatures: "From the point of view of Genesis 1 or the 104th Psalm, we would say that all are of one kind, one kinship, one nature, because all are *creatures*."[2]

In one of his most important essays on the subject, "Health Is Membership," Berry explores what it means to be healthy. "To be healthy is literally to be whole," he writes. Noting the word's etymological connection to "holy," he goes on to say that any proper healer should "respect the holiness embodied in all creatures, or that our healing involves the preservation in us of the spirit and the breath of God."[3] To be healthy is then to preserve our givenness and connection, to live into the proper balance of our dependence upon God and the creation of which we are a part.

As we've already noted in previous chapters, this reality is one that is bound through love, all of it turning on affection. Berry writes:

I take literally the statement in the Gospel of John that God loves the world. I believe that the world was created and approved by love, that it subsists, coheres, and endures by love, and that, insofar as it is redeemable, it can be redeemed only by love. I believe that divine love, incarnate and indwelling in the world, summons the world always toward wholeness, which ultimately is reconciliation and atonement with God.[4]

To be a member then is to be a part of something God is doing in the world, a gathering together that comes through the incarnation. It is a making right through reconciliation.

With love and givenness as the conditions of our health, the fundamental realities of our being, it makes no sense to treat the health of person as an individual in isolation. For Berry it is "community—in the fullest sense: a place and all its creatures"—that is the smallest unit of health. This is why in the fiction story "Fidelity" Danny breaks his father Burley free from his isolation in the hospital and brings him home. In the hospital, Burley is diseased, disconnected from the membership in which he is healthy. When he is back at home, even though he dies, he dies in health because he does so being connected and in place.

In a similar vein, Berry reflects on the experience of his brother John undergoing bypass surgery after a heart attack. While thankful for the medical treatment his brother received, Berry is struck by the obstacles to care inherent in the hospital system. "In the hospital what I will call the world of love meets the world of efficiency," Berry writes, "the world, that is, of specialization, machinery and abstract procedure."[5] The two worlds run parallel in place, like the city of God and man, but they are not aimed at the same ends—one is driven by the modes of analysis which divide, dissect, and separate while the other works in the modes of affection which link and join.

This work of love is rooted in the divine love, but it must live in the realities of mortality, the inescapable limits of "ignorance and partiality." "Like divine love, earthly love seeks plentitude; it longs for the full membership to be present and to be joined," writes Berry. "Unlike divine love, earthly love does not have the power, the knowledge, or the will to achieve what it longs for."[6] Our mortal love always fails, it is always incomplete, yet guided in its desire to complete itself, it seeks to expand and include more and more in its membership.

This impulse is represented powerfully in the example of the "shepherd, [who] owning a hundred sheep and having lost one, does not say, 'I have saved 99 percent of my sheep,' but rather, 'I have lost one,' and he goes and searches for the one."[7] In his short story, "Watch with Me," Berry illustrates how this care looks in a community.

The story follows a mentally ill man in the community of Port William nicknamed "Nightlife" for his periodic night wanderings around the countryside. One evening at a revival meeting, Nightlife tells the minister that God has told him to preach. The minister responds that he cannot preach, and, when rebuffed, Nightlife "throwed a reg'lar fit."[8] Being the largest man at the gathering and a neighbor of Nightlife's family, Ptolemy Proudfoot is called upon to calm the man and send him home.

The next day, Nightlife comes to Proudfoot's farm, steals his gun, and threatens to commit suicide. As the story progresses, Proudfoot follows Nightlife as he begins wandering around the community, armed and as though in a daze. Along the way, a band of others join in the cautious, careful parade behind this deranged man with a loaded gun.

After a storm drives the men inside, Nightlife cradling his gun as though ready to shoot, begins the revival service he intended to lead all along. He leads the men in a hymn and then begins his sermon on Matthew 18:12 about the shepherd who leaves the ninety-nine in search of the one "gone astray." "Though Christ, in speaking this parable, asked his hearers to think of the shepherd," the narrator says, "Nightlife understood it entirely from the viewpoint of the lost sheep."[9] And, as readers, we come to see that it is this parable that has been playing out over the story. The men of the Port William membership have been following this lost sheep among them, seeking to find and restore him. After the sermon, Nightlife comes back to himself and Proudfoot is able to take back his gun. The threat of violent rupture is passed and the one lost is restored to the community.

This theme of reconciliation, of restoring those lost to the community, is a theme at the heart of the Christian Gospel. Many of Jesus's acts of healing were oriented around diseases such as leprosy that isolated people, cutting them off from the rest of society. There is likely no more disconnecting disease in our day than mental illness, as Berry's story wisely indicates. But for the work of reconciliation to make sense, for reconciliation to mean anything, there must be a membership to which we can be reconciled. It is the discovery of this membership and our recollection within it that is perhaps the greatest challenge for many of us in this age of easy travel and disconnected lives.

• • •

The work of membership to join what has been broken and disconnected by industrial society is the theme of Berry's remarkable short novel, *Remembering*. It is a novel about Andy Catlett, a character many readers see as a not too distant corollary to Berry himself. Catlett is a farmer and a farm journalist, who has taken up the cause of small farmers against the industrialists who promote the doctrine of "get big or get out." But in this novel, we find him wounded, suffering the physical and psychological damage that has come from the loss of an arm. He has literally been dismembered by agricultural machinery, and with that disconnection, he has fallen into a despair that has separated him from his wife and his community.

In the novel, we find Catlett in San Francisco, a place with which Berry is familiar, having completed his study of writing there under Wallace Stegner at Stanford. The character Andy is there to speak at a conference on agriculture, to voice his dissent for the policies of industrialization being promoted there (recalling Berry's own debates with Earl Butz, Nixon's Secretary of Agriculture). But while he is defending his community, he feels its absence. He finds himself in the anonymous space of a hotel room, alone and away: "A man could go so far from home, he thinks, that his own name would become unspeakable by him, unanswerable by anyone, so that if he dared to speak it, it would escape him utterly, a bird out an open window, leaving him untongued in some boundless amplitude of mere absence."[10]

This absence and anonymity are the attraction of cities to many and Andy feels its draw. It is in these places, free from the communities in which they became themselves that many people seek to be unbound. "All distance is around him, and he wants nothing that he has," writes Berry. "All choice is around him, and he knows nothing that he wants."[11] But in the end, Catlett does not feel the anonymous city as a place of liberation; it contains for him the same ache of loneliness and absence he feels in the ghost of his lost arm.

Unable to sleep, Catlett goes for a walk through the early morning of San Francisco. It is along this journey that he begins to remember and be re-membered—to be drawn back toward wholeness and health by reentering the community in which he is complete. As he walks, he begins to recall the many people and places of his life. Lost in the vastness of the city, he begins to find himself through recollection—the stories of the Port William membership that span beyond the borders of his own lifetime.

His walk complete, Andy is shuttled to the airport. The gates offer a choice of elsewhere, other places he could go, but not places to which he could return. Still unsettled, he boards the flight home. When he finally arrives, his family is gone to the neighbors' and so he takes a moment to rest, but again his sleep is not restful. He realizes in his sleep that "what he is, all that he is…is a nothing possessed of a terrible self-knowledge."[12] But Andy is not left there, "from outside his hopeless dark sleep a touch is laid upon his shoulder." A man appears and guides him through the familiar countryside of his home place, but it is a place that "though it is familiar to him, is changed." There is a radiant quality to the place he is now moving through, it is a place filled with "the song of the many members of one love."[13]

Andy is able to see in this transformed Port William and its countryside "the signs everywhere upon them of the care of a longer love than any who have lived there have ever imagined."[14] It is a place teeming with people, "resting and talking together in the peace of a Sabbath profound and bright."[15] He realizes "that these are the membership of one another and of the place and of the song or light in which they live and move." It is a vision of heaven, but this heaven is not elsewhere. It is here, made complete and whole. The plentitude made limited by human fallenness has been fulfilled; a place where living and dead, all that was and is are together "and nothing is lost."[16] It is a beatific vision in which Andy is able to see the membership, built through the long loves of its people and place, fulfilled through the divine love that makes it complete. In this vision, though he still bares the wound of his damaged arm, Andy is restored to wholeness.

• • •

This possibility of wholeness is the gift membership offers to us—a gift we cannot accept without it. So long as we refuse to join in the communion of the whole creation, we cannot hope to be anything but partial, damaged, and isolated. But when we link our lives to the membership we begin to join a wholeness that no one of us can even begin to comprehend or imagine. We begin to be a part of a completeness that is beyond us.

Writing about how good work joins us to the membership, Berry compares our connection with the whole to a person entering a communal dance moving in concentric circles. "We enter the little circle of each other's arms," he writes, "and the larger circle of all creatures, passing in and out of life, who move also in a dance, to a music so subtle and vast that no ear hears it except in fragments."[17]

In joining this dance, however, it is important that we stay ourselves. To be a part of the membership is not to live into conformity, but rather to find the freedom to be fully oneself. There is a kind of paradox at play here, but it is a truth I have found borne out in my own experience. I've known many who have lived in various forms of intentional communities from traditional monasteries to communes born from the 1960s Jesus People movements. Of all the people I've known, these have been the most unique and varied, expressing the full range of human personality and possibility. In his Port William membership, Berry expresses the same truth. The people of Port William are hardly conformist—each one is fully a "character."

To be a part of the membership is antithetical to isolation, but not to solitude. Solitude is in fact a key feature of our creaturely lives—a way in which we come to be fully responsive to the lives of others. For Berry, "True solitude is found in the wild places, where one is without human obligation." It is by being in such wild places that we are able to retune our ears to hear the subtle music of the dance of all creation. "The more coherent one becomes within oneself as a creature," he writes, "the more fully one enters into the communion of all creatures."[18]

For the human creature, the coherence born of membership not only comes from renewal in wild places, but also "a cultural cycle in harmony with the fertility cycle" of creation.[19] This cultural cycle is "an unending conversation between old people and young people, assuring the survival of local memory, which has, as long as it remains local, the greatest practical urgency and value."[20] It is the preservation of this cycle that "is meant, and is all that can be meant, by 'sustainability.'"[21] That such cultural cycles are hard to find in modern industrial societies illustrates just how unsustainable such societies are. The best examples of working sustainable cultures are those indigenous societies that have been able to hold on to this conversation in their places. Athabascan Native communities for instance, despite great pressures, have been able to continue important knowledge about how to live in the wilderness of Alaska. Such cultures and the sustainability they represent are under constant threat.

Berry illustrates this work of local culture in his place through the example and metaphor of an old bucket that hangs from a fence on what was his grandfather's farm. The bucket has been hanging there for as long as Berry can remember, and, over the years, it has collected leaves and water and animal droppings, forming a rich layer of soil. But beyond leaves, "It collects stories, too, as they fall through time." It has become a part of the history of the place, and it has become a part of the place's story. "It is doing in a passive way what a human community must do actively and thoughtfully," Berry writes, "A human community, too, must collect leaves and stories, and turn them to account. It must build soil, and build that memory of itself—in lore and story and song—that will be its culture."[22]

This work is the work of the membership, a work that seeks to know and make sense of its place as well as move toward its flourishing. This is why the local culture cannot be simply a thing on display in concert venues and art galleries, but something that will "preserve and improve the local soil." If it fails at this then "the local community will decay and perish."[23]

All of this sounds fine and good, I'm sure. The question for many of us is how to translate this vision to our places, places already covered over in concrete, obscured by the anonymity of strip malls. Can we too have a membership even in the hyper mobile spaces in which we find ourselves? For those of us who grew up in multiple places and never knew the kind of life Port William represents, can we be a part of such a robust community of creation?

The answer, as Berry has on occasion said, is that we must begin. We must make a start. A good place to begin this work is to meet our neighbors, human and wild, and to learn our neighborhoods in all their variety. After meeting our community, we should become neighbors, starting the work of sharing life in our places.

We should also work toward the cultivation of our local cultures. In my own city, this cultivation is beginning to flourish around farmers markets and clusters of small shops that are energizing one another other. These are places where local musicians gather, punk rockers sitting to hear bluegrass strummers (both of which have a strong local history here) and cowboy-booted farmers chat forage with Californians who decided to stop and stay here for good. Local culture also flourishes around poetry readings, handmade chap books, and local films. These are people making culture for their neighbors with no ambitions for an audience beyond them. It is local culture that happens in kitchens when traditional foods are prepared with local ingredients taking on the twists of the seasons.

A flourishing membership, a place where culture and agriculture are interlinked with the local people and landscape, is one in which the centers of import and export begin to diminish their roles. Los Angeles and New York have their place, but if they were to both be swallowed by the rising seas (as well they could) the local culture would still have its means of reflecting, mourning, celebrating, and understanding in a way that is tied to its place. For Berry, this is what true diversity looks like—many places living in their many varieties rather than submitting to monoculture.

To be a member of a place, we must be embodied and entangled in it, we must share and learn the lessons of the place. There is no general map for how this might happen. Each place will necessarily have its own way. But to begin, we must go, get "out of your car, off your horse," and belong somewhere.

CHAPTER NINE

The Body and the Earth

. . . .

RECLAIMING CONNECTION IN A WORLD OF DIVISION

It is said that when Rene Descartes, one of the philosophical fathers of modern science, vivisected a dog (that is, dissected it alive), he paid no attention to its cries. He didn't bother with any anesthesia for the animal; it was, to his mind, merely a machine. It had no soul, no real spirit—the whimpers and howls the dog let out as it was cut open were to Descartes like the creaking of an ungreased wheel.

This is quite a different view than that of the psalmist who saw the breath of God as the breath of life—no different whether human or animal. An ancient Hebrew might kill an animal, but he would never pretend that it was without a spirit. He knew, and felt beholden to the knowledge, that this was another creature of God's making and God's breath: "When you take away their breath, they die and return to their dust. When you send for your spirit they are created; and you renew the face of the ground" (Psalm 104:29b–30).

We would like to think that we are better than Descartes, more "enlightened" than this founding member of the Enlightenment, but our common attitudes are closer to Descartes's than to the psalmist's. Go to any grocery store, and you will see the proof. The meat there, most of it (if not *all of it* in any conventional store), will be from animals raised in spaces not unlike factories. The animals will have been regarded as "production units" and "protein solutions," but never as living things other than their basic needs for water, food, and enough health to make it to slaughter. Most of this meat is disguised, separated from the animals to which the flesh once belonged. For a time, I raised chickens on pasture and sold them at a farmers market. I had customers complain from time to time that these whole chickens looked too much like chickens. This is where we are.

The human bodies that this meat of animal machines will feed will be treated little differently. They too will be regarded as machines, spirited machines, but machines all the same. The human person was to Descartes's mind and many after him a divided reality—an eternal soul and a machine-like body. Only the soul was of any importance—the body simply required regular maintenance, like a car.

E.O. Wilson, a scientist based at Harvard whose book *Consilience* prompted Berry to write *Life is a Miracle: An Essay Against Modern Superstition*, echoes Descartes's model, but would delete the soul from the equation. A thoroughgoing naturalist, Wilson writes that, "People…are just extremely complicated machines."[1] It is this reduction of creaturely life that Berry sees as the heart of our problem. By reducing creatures to machines, Berry writes that we have been willing "to allow machines and the idea of the machine to prescribe the terms and conditions of the lives of creatures, which we have allowed increasingly for the last two centuries, and are still allowing, at an incalculable cost to other creatures *and to ourselves.*"[2] This damage is clear in the factory farms where animals are treated as machines, breaking away from any humane standard of care. It is also clear in those who eat such animals, their own health damaged by the machine model that denies our common creaturely life.

All of this damage results from a reduction which like a value fixed in a dollar price, makes the creature merely a material thing and therefore something that can be traded easily in a market. As Berry writes, "the scientific-industrial culture, founded nominally upon materialism, arrives at a sort of fundamental disdain for material reality. The living world is then treated as dead matter, the worth of which is determined exclusively by the market."[3]

Such materialism, the natural outcome of the division of body from soul, not only gives way to the reduction of animals to machines, but also carries with it a kind of contempt for the body that is less than the soul. It is easy, once the body has been divided from the soul, to say that some bodies are without spirit. This then lends itself to the possibility of slavery and other exploitations of the body. "Contempt for the body is invariably manifested in contempt for other bodies—the bodies of slaves, laborers, women, animals, plants, the earth itself," writes Berry. "Relationships with all other creatures become competitive and exploitive rather than collaborative and convivial."[4]

This separation of the body from the soul, from its mysterious life and breath (spirit), leads inevitably to disease and unrest. "Our bodies have become marginal," writes Berry, "they are growing useless like our 'marginal' land because we have less and less use for them. After the games and idle flourishes of modern youth, we use them only as shipping cartons to transport our brains and our few employable muscles back and forth to work."[5]

But rather than working to reconnect our bodies within the whole of the creation, restoring soul and place and membership to their life, our modern "health" systems rely on the same machine metaphors, the same divisions and reductions that began the disease.

"Where the art and science of healing are concerned, the machine metaphor works to enforce a division that falsifies the process of healing because it falsifies the nature of the creature needing to be healed," writes Berry. "If the body is a machine, then its disease can be healed by a sort of mechanical tinkering, without reference to anything outside the body itself."[6]

Without such outside reference, the body is left alone—disconnected from the community, soul, friendships, creatures, and contexts in which it can be whole. "To try to heal the body alone is to collaborate in the destruction of the body," Berry writes. "Healing is impossible in loneliness; it is the opposite of loneliness. Conviviality is healing. To be healed we must come with all the other creatures to the feast of Creation."[7]

This is an insight that is being confirmed at the margins of science as our medical advances are beginning to run up against a host of "modern" diseases, once unknown and still rare in places without the benefits of our sterilized and divided existence. Though our understanding is still limited, it is becoming clear that for the body to be healthy we must live with other organisms—to be connected to and even hosts to them. On the most basic level this comes in a move toward consuming "probiotics," bacteria and fungi that aid in everything from digestion to our mental health.[8] This is to speak only of the most intimate of our relationships with other creatures. As we have already explored, Berry is right to say that health is membership.

To be separated from this membership, our bodies take on a joyless existence, formed not toward their flourishing, but on the basis of external models. We are dissatisfied with our bodies, not as they have become through disuse, but as they were given. We have accepted the standards of the advertisers over the standards of health, the measure that we learn only through communion with creation and the ongoing conversation between body and soul. "The body is degraded and saddened by being set in conflict against the creation itself, of which all bodies are members, therefore members of each other," writes Berry. "The body is thus sent to war against itself."[9] So it is that blood panels and magazine racks define our well-being and beauty for us. We no longer have a sense for what health feels like because we have been so alienated from the membership that is its source.

● ● ●

Our religion, as is commonly practiced and taught, is of little help. Though Christianity from its earliest days struggled against the Gnostic sects that sought to coopt it, this perversion remains a persistent temptation. The Gnostics were, like Descartes, dualists—separating the world into the spiritual and the material. The spiritual was good, the sphere of freedom and wisdom, while the material world was evil, the source of our pain and folly.

The Gnostics, as early Christians soon realized, posed a problem for a people who worshipped a God who created the world and called it good, became flesh, and was resurrected in the body. Nonetheless, Christians have never been able to fully shake the Gnostic heresy. It has the appeal of escape rather than redemption for this world. Rather than a renewed heavens and a renewed earth, it promises "sweet heaven by and by, way up in the sky."

Modern religion has become characterized by this perversion, so much so that there are whole swaths of Christians who believe that care for the earth or body matter little since they'll all be shed after all. "This separation of the soul from the body and from the world is no disease of the fringe, no aberration, but a fracture that runs through the mentality of institutional religion like a geologic fault," writes Berry. "And this rift in the mentality of religion continues to characterize the modern mind, no matter how secular or worldly it becomes."[10]

To return us to the healing connections of the body to the earth and the body to the soul, we must not only address modern science, but also renew ancient religion. And though one can find many examples of religion contributing to this separation, one can find sources for cohesion and completeness in the best of Christian theology and in the Bible. Pope Francis's work in *Laudato Si'*, for instance, has helped move us away from dichotomies and toward an "integral" theology. He has shown that religion can play a key role in protecting from the modern temptation to have absolute power over creation. As he writes in *Laudato Si'*:

> The acceptance of our bodies as God's gift is vital for welcoming and accepting the entire world as a gift from the Father and our common home, whereas thinking that

we enjoy absolute power over our own bodies turns, often subtly, into thinking that we enjoy absolute power over creation.[11]

This preservation of the idea of gift means religion should, properly, be on the side of mystery—it should stand against the reduction of the world because part of the religious impulse and task is to always insist that there is more. But dualism violates this preservation of mystery. As Berry writes, "dualism inevitably reduces physical reality, and it does so by removing its mystery from it, by dividing it absolutely from what dualistic thinkers have understood as spiritual or mental reality."[12] By joining in dualism, religion has set up the conditions for its demise—once spirit is separated from the material reality it is also easily deleted. But such separation need not happen, in fact it should not, if we are thinking along with the Hebrew and Christian scriptures.

"I believe that the Creation is one continuous fabric comprehending simultaneously what we mean by 'spirit' and what we mean by 'matter,'" writes Berry.[13] This is a holistic vision of reality and one that Berry comes to not in spite of the Bible, but from it. "The Bible's aim, as I read it, is not the freeing of the spirit from the world," Berry answers to the Gnostic impulse. "It is the handbook of their interaction. It says that they cannot be divided; that their mutuality, their unity, is inescapable; that they are not reconciled in division, but in harmony."[14] We can find such a vision of reconciled harmony in the famous hymn in Colossians in which Christ is proclaimed as the one "pleased to reconcile to himself all things, whether on earth or in heaven, by making peace through the blood of the lamb" (Colossians

1:20). We can find it again in Romans when St. Paul writes that "the whole creation has been groaning in labor pains," awaiting a common redemption with all things (see Romans 8:18–25). These are not messages of redemption by means of an evacuation of souls from the realm of earthly creation. What Berry finds in the Bible, we should too: a handbook of interaction and harmony between the whole of created reality, soul and body, body and earth.

• • •

After shaking ourselves free of false dualisms and divisions, how do we come to understand the truth of our connections and ourselves? How do we come to live into them? One of the directions Berry points us toward is an embrace of our limits; a renewal of our life as humus living from and dependent on the soil. "The question of human limits, of the proper definition and place of human beings within the order of Creation, finally rests upon our attitude toward our biological existence, the life of the body in this world," he writes.[15] If we want to live our lives within our proper order, then we must pay attention to our bodily life in this world, we must embrace the measure of a human scale.

To live into this scale we should gain a sense of our lives within the vastness of creation. Berry talks of Chinese landscape paintings in which tiny human figures move against a backdrop of vast mountains. The value of wild places, of landscapes free of human cultivation and control, is to help remind us of this scale. To go backpacking in a wilderness isn't simply an adventure or exercise in exploratory conquest. It is a time in which we can be reminded of the distance of miles apart from cars, the burden of carrying what we need on our backs without machines, the vast life of the forests in which a human being is only a curiosity to be scolded by foraging chickadees.

Unfortunately, too many people's interaction with the wild comes trained by the confines of human control, a step beyond proper limits. When we drive to the top of Cadillac Mountain in Acadia National Park on the Maine coast, we miss the full power of its height, our smallness against its vastness. Tragically, reminders of the wild sometimes come when the forces of nature conflict with the safe zones of domesticity. When a child was drowned by an alligator at a pond in Disney World, we were reminded of something our forbearers knew commonly—that we too can be prey, that human lives for all of our control can be victims of a nature that includes us and is beyond us.

"Past the scale of the human, our works do not liberate us— they confine us," writes Berry. "They cut off access to the wilderness of Creation where we must go to be reborn—to receive the awareness, at once humbling and exhilarating, grievous and joyful, that we are a part of Creation, one with all that we live from and all that, in turn, lives from us."[16] Between joy and grief, this is the reality of the body, it is the reality of the creation of which we are a part. It is in isolation that this joy and grief is tragic, but as we move toward the given world our sorrow and our joy can return to the feast of creation and the abundant life of God. Our divisions and wounds can live in the hope of healing, the health of wholeness—heaven come to earth.

"When Jesus speaks of having life more abundantly, this, I think, is the life He means," writes Berry, "a life that is not reducible by division, category, or degree, but is one thing, heavenly and earthly, spiritual and material, divided only insofar as it is embodied in distinct creatures."[17] We can begin to live this life through the sacramental efforts of work—the engagements with the creation by which we come to see that every place is fundamentally what the Celts called a "thin place," a space in which heaven is near to earth and earth near to heaven.

For Berry, one of the necessary forms of work by which humankind can live into this sacrament is in the growing of food. When we grow food, we are enacting the truth that: "While we live our bodies are moving particles of the earth, joined inextricably both to the soil and to the bodies of other living creatures."[18] By working the soil and growing food from it, we are participating in "a sacrament, as eating is also, by which we enact and understand our oneness with the Creation, the conviviality of one body with all bodies."[19]

By growing food, we make connections and shorten the distance between them. To eat a tomato grown from my own garden is to receive the product of work but also the gift of grace, and as such, it reminds me of this exchange of gifts in all creation. Our work only ever goes so far; we are dependent upon the work of worms and microbes, we are dependent upon the work of rot and compost, we are dependent on the slow work of wind and rain, the movements of silt and sand over the eons of geologic time. And we are dependent too on our work, on our care in balance with these gifts. We hunger as we work and at the end of the work our hunger is satisfied—we grow food and we eat it.

This is what all good work should do. It should connect us— bodies and souls, creatures and creation. This connection is not simply a support for a disconnected life, but instead *is* life.

"Good work is not just the maintenance of connections—as one is now said to work 'for a living' or 'to support a family'—but the *enactment* of connections," writes Berry. "It *is* living, and a way of living; it is not support for a family in the sense of an exterior brace or prop, but is one of the forms and acts of love."[20]

Love is the life of gift; it is as St. Paul says (1 Corinthians 13)—patient, kind, never insisting on its own way. Work as love, in the way of love, must then also embrace patience, kindness, and generosity. Hasty work that seeks to turn a profit today on a product that will soon be gone does nothing to bring the body home, it uses the body as a "tool" just as it uses the world—converting the creation into abstract cash. Good work uses the world and our bodies, it employees them, but it is directed toward connection, toward the settled life of home. "We are working well when we use ourselves as the fellow creatures of the plants, animals, materials, and other people we are working with," writes Berry. "Such work is unifying, healing. It brings us home from pride and from despair, and places us responsibly within the human estate. It defines us as we are: not too good to work with our bodies, but too good to work poorly or joylessly or selfishly or alone."[21]

Good work gives the body pleasure, a reality that has always accompanied love and connection. Good work also gives the body rest because it allows it to live in the grace of the world. "Where is our comfort but in the free, uninvolved, finally mysterious beauty and grace of this world that we did not make, that has no price?" asks Berry. "Where is our pleasure but in working and resting kindly in the presence of this world?"[22] It is in the work of our bodies that we are able to find our living connection with the creation and it is with pleasure that we find that connection lovely.

As with all else, the body's truth turns on affection and this affection is the final break with any dichotomy or reduction. "A body, love insists, is neither a spirit nor a machine; it is not a picture, a diagram, a chart, a graph, an anatomy; it is not an explanation; it is not a law," writes Berry. "It is precisely and uniquely what it is. It belongs to the world of love, which is a world of living creatures, natural orders and cycles, many small, fragile lights in the dark."[23] So it is that the body belongs not to itself or another, but to a whole, a membership in which it finds its fullest expression in the harmony of a dance. As Berry's poetic persona "the Mad Farmer" calls in the poem "The Mad Farmer, Flying the Flag of Rough Branch, Secedes from the Union":

> Come into the life of the body, the one body
> granted to you in all the history of time.
> Come into the body's economy, its day work,
> and its replenishment at mealtimes and at night.
> Come into the body's thanksgiving, when it knows
> and acknowledges itself a living soul.
> Come into the dance of community, joined
> in a circle, hand in hand, the dance of the eternal
> love of women and men for one another
> and of neighbors and friends for one another.[24]

Come into the body. It is here that we must live if we are to become again what we were made and given, creatures born of love.

CHAPTER TEN

Language

· · · · · · · · · · · · · · · · · ·

TRUTH AND THE WORK OF IMAGINATION

Several years ago, the agribusiness company Monsanto, a pioneer in pesticides and genetically modified crops, began a new public-relations campaign. Led by the PR firm Edelman, Monsanto sought to brand itself as a company dedicated to sustainable agriculture. Through National Public Radio sponsorships, press releases, and a campaign to win over bloggers, Monsanto represented itself as a company at the forefront of fighting hunger and climate change through the development of drought resistant corn, soybeans, and cotton. They promised to develop such crops in the next thirty years.

The problem was that Monsanto's vision of "sustainability" was in stark contrast to the forms of agriculture that have, in fact, proved sustainable over long periods of time. Theirs was a vision for the future with no roots in the past. The kinds of seeds they were promoting were for crop varieties that are questionable (addressing food shortages means more crop varieties, not more soybeans and corn) and would require heavy machinery and significant chemical pesticide and fertilizer inputs. This is not to mention that farmers growing these crops would be unable to save their seeds for the next generation. Instead, they would have to purchase seeds annually from Monsanto along with the licenses to grow the company's patented crops. One would have a hard time applying the word "sustainable" to such an enterprise unless one was not very careful with language, or more so, calculating in the undermining of its meaning, its truth.

That one would rarely find Wendell Berry using the word "sustainable" or especially "sustainable agriculture" is telling. Berry is deeply sensitive to language and to the possibility of language to lie. For him, words and phrases like "sustainable" or "organic" or "climate change" are all vulnerable to manipulation. Instead, Berry has sought to accept the gift of language, to submit to it rather than master it, submitting all the more to the truth that stands with and behind the words. After reflecting on the gifts of creation and human culture, Berry writes in his poem "Some Further Words":

> ...My purpose,
> is a language that can pay just thanks
> and honor for those gifts, a tongue
> set free from fashionable lies.[1]

. . .

"Don't lie"—the theologian Stanley Hauerwas has said that the whole of Christian ethics can be summed up in those two words. It is a provocative statement, but it has a strong tradition behind it. St. Augustine held an absolute prohibition on lying, forbidding even what some would consider a "noble lie" to save another. Augustine believed that withholding information was just fine, but that when one speaks, one must speak truthfully.

Aquinas likewise believed that lying was always wrong because it presented a central conflict with the truthful self. One cannot lie and be a person of integrity—the lie dissolves one's integrity. German theologian Dietrich Bonhoeffer, a man who died at the hands of the Nazis because of his involvement in an assassination plot against Hitler, was among the most adamant proponents of truthful language. "Bonhoeffer," writes Hauerwas, "was a relentless critic of any way of life that substituted agreeableness for truthfulness."[2] Bonhoeffer's relentless commitment to the truth made its question central to the life of the church, even in the smallest matters. It is this truth against small concessions and compromise that is the path toward faithful witness in the world. As Hauerwas writes further:

> I think Bonhoeffer rightly saw that the Christian acceptance that truth does not matter in such small matters prepared the ground for the terrible lie that was Hitler. In order to expose the small as well as the big lies a community must exist that has learned to speak truthfully to one another. That community, moreover, must know that to speak truthfully to one another requires the time granted through the work of forgiveness. Such patient timefulness is a gift from the God the community believes has given us all the time we need to care for the words we speak to one another.[3]

An important aspect of Berry's work that has been often overlooked and yet is central is that he is a writer worried about his words—he is careful with and of them, but this isn't simply because he wants to clearly communicate or elicit a particular emotion or response. His care is rooted in his desire to be truthful in his language and thus in himself. This truthfulness relies on the meeting both of the world and community of which he is a part and the person he is as writer and speaker.

Quoting Thoreau, Berry writes, "where would you look for standard English but to the words of a standard man?"[4] It is an exploration of this relationship between language and character, person and the place that animates Berry's important essay "Standing By Words."

Berry begins the essay by arguing that language has a responsibility to reality; it is measured against a truth that is greater than the writer or poet. This is the sense he finds in the "old poets." "The truth the poet chose as his subject," writes Berry, "was perceived as *superior* to his powers—and, by clear implication, to his occasion and purpose."[5] To write was then a fearful thing, not in the negative sense, but in the sense of working with a power well beyond oneself. The poet had to be careful with words because the truth the poet was expressing was greater than the poet herself.

Such a way of understanding language requires that the poet become a certain kind of person. The kind of person that is able to "stand by one's words." As Berry writes, "The idea of standing by one's word, of words precisely designating things, of deeds faithful to words, is probably native to our understanding. Indeed, it seems doubtful that we could understand anything without that idea."[6] Language relies on a certain kind of truthfulness—it relies on a correspondence between the words and their objects, and it relies on a consistency between the speaker and the words spoken, the writer and the words laid down.

We must note here that this does not mean that the writer necessarily lives up to his words in all ways. It is possible, and more than probable that a writer can see and say a truth without being able to fully live into that truth. Berry is not saying that a writer must be perfect in order to tell the truth. His poem "A Warning to My Readers" makes the case beautifully:

Do not think me gentle
because I speak in praise
of gentleness, or elegant
because I honor the grace
that keeps this world. I am
a man crude as any,
gross of speech, intolerant,
stubborn, angry, full
of fits and furies. That I
may have spoken well
at times, is not natural.
A wonder is what it is.[7]

To have spoken well, to have told the truth, is again something that comes not from the poet's powers, but from his ability to properly receive a gift given. This is part of what being subject to our subject means. But this grace does not mean that our words can exist truthfully without action or that they can at the very least be judged independent of our actions.

Berry ties this link between action and word to the "Christian idea of the Incarnate Word." In this idea "the Word [enters] the world as flesh, and inevitably therefore as action—which leads logically enough to the insistence in the epistle of James that faith without works is dead."[8] We may not always live up to our words, but to speak without an accompanying action is bound to prove untruthful in some way.

We cannot simply speak with any action, however. Truthful language must always remain connected to a context and community in which it is made meaningful. All truthful language is rooted in a kind of community speech "in which words live in the presence of their objects," writes Berry.[9] When language becomes "cut off from this source," Berry writes, "language becomes a paltry work of conscious purpose, at the service and mercy of expedient aims."[10] This is the language one often finds in bureaucracies and business—senseless jargon that only makes sense in its reduction of a mysterious and rich reality. This is the sort of language that drives the ambitions of industry, uninterested in accepting the value of the world and set instead on making it; subjecting its subject rather than being subject to it. Berry compares such efforts to the biblical story of Babel, where people attempted to reach the heavens with a tower. "It is perhaps a law of human nature," writes Berry," that such ambition always produces a confusion of tongues."[11]

To escape this sort of confusion, to stand by our words, we must find a kind of balance between the inner and outer aspects of ourselves. "When my awareness of how I feel overpowers my awareness of where I am and who is there with me, I am sick, diseased," writes Berry.[12] We cannot be entirely internal persons, dwelling within ourselves to the degree that we cannot communicate with others about any general feeling. Berry points to some of the poems of Byron as an example of this—they are so wrought with the internal emotion of the poet that they fail to communicate to any other person.

"The converse is also true," writes Berry. "I am diseased if I become so aware of my surroundings that my own inward life is obscured, as if I should so fix upon the value of some mineral in the ground as to forget that the world is God's work and my home."[13] This is the threat of bureaucrats, most terribly expressed in cases where some crime is committed by someone "simply doing my job." For language to function, it must dance between the inner and outer, it must bring the self home.

"Persons are joined to families, families to communities," writes Berry, "by disciplines that must be deliberately made, remembered, taught, learned, and practiced."[14] Truthful language connects us and it must be deliberate, but it must also avoid being so exact as to exclude the mystery of reality. It must always be tenuous enough that any word can never be taken to be complete or final. This is part of what religion provides to language. "The practical use of religion," writes Berry, "is to keep the accounting [of language] in as large a context as possible—to see in fact that the account is never 'closed.'"[15] Religion maintains the "unsolvable X" that keeps the balances of costs and benefits, debits and credits unsolvable so that no final profit can be declared. Religion, in other words, keeps us careful with our words by preserving their mystery.

I am reminded here again of the parallels with Bonhoeffer. In a speech to a youth ecumenical gathering, he said:

> No good at all can come from acting before the world and one's self as though we knew the truth, when in reality we do not. This truth is too important for that, and it would be a betrayal of this truth if the church were to hide itself behind resolutions and pious so-called

Christian principles, when it is called to look the truth in the face and once and for all confess its guilt and ignorance. Indeed, such resolutions can have nothing complete, nothing clear about them unless the whole Christian truth, as the church knows it or confesses that it does not know it, stands behind them. Qualified silence might perhaps be more appropriate for the church today than talk which is very unqualified. That means protest against any form of the church which does not honour the question of truth above all things.[16]

Silence is often the only truthful speech we can muster if we are to remain truthful to the mystery. As a poet Berry is well aware that what is said is always best when surrounded by the many things unsaid. He writes in the closing stanza of his poem "How to Be a Poet *(to remind myself)*":

Accept what comes from silence.
Make the best you can of it.
Of the little words that come
out of the silence, like prayers
prayed back to the one who prays,
make a poem that does not disturb
the silence from which it came.[17]

The importance of silence comes from the need to be "subject to our subject." Our work is judged not by our powers or virtuosity (the kind of genius sought by Byron), but by the ability of our work to fit within the given world of which our given lives are a part. This is why Berry writes that he seeks to "make a poem that does not disturb / the silence from which it came."

In "Standing By Words" he writes that this ability of work to fit is the true judge of its quality. "The quality of work or of a made thing would be determined by how conservingly it fitted into the system of systems," writes Berry. "Judgment could then begin to articulate what is already obvious: that some work preserves the household of life, and some work destroys it."[18]

For Berry, language must then be proprietary, which is to say, appropriate: "the tool to the work, the work to the need, the need to other needs and the needs of others, and to the health of the household or community of all creatures."[19] Such work stands in contrast to the work of power that seeks to force the world to submit to its will. There is a certain aesthetic of power that celebrates the submission of the creation rather than being subject to it. This is rooted in part in our modern conceptions of the creative genius—the person who creates out of nothing, breaking with all that was before. But such raw power and creativity are no more beautiful than the work done in quiet submission to the standards of form. "The elaborations of elegance," writes Berry, "are at least as fascinating, and more various, more democratic, more healthy, more practiced—though less glamorous—than elaborations of power."[20]

Berry offers an example of the difference between these two aesthetics in his essay "Style and Grace." It is an essay that works through a comparison of two river fishing stories: Hemingway's "Big Two-hearted River" and Norman Maclean's "A River Runs through It." Berry praises Hemingway's story for what he sees "to be a triumph of style in its pure and purifying sense: the ability to isolate those parts of experience of which one can confidently take charge."[21] But such a style, by seeking to master, has severe limits and dangers. "The problem with style of this kind," writes Berry, "is that it is severely reductive of both humanity and nature…. Like the similarly reductive technical and professional specializations of our time, this style minimizes to avoid mystery. It deals with what it does not understand by leaving it out."[22]

In contrast to this reduction, Berry find's Maclean's "A River Runs through It" to exhibit the opposite kind of style. Rather than a style that seeks mastery and therefore avoids what it cannot master, "A River Runs through It" is written in a style "vulnerable to bewilderment, mystery, and tragedy—and a style, therefore, that is open to grace."[23] It is a story that connects and fits itself within the larger life of larger truths: "Reading it, we are not allowed to forget that we are dealing with immortal principles and affections, and with the lives of immortal souls."[24]

Hemingway's style, in comparison, "like a victorious general, imposes its terms on its subject."[25] In so doing, it exhibits its art, "conscious of it as a feat of style."[26] In contrast, the art at work in "A River Runs through It" "seems to be a used, rather than an exhibited, art, one that ultimately subjects itself to its subject."[27]

●　●　●

Language, for Berry, is connected to the work of imagination, which is indeed an ingredient in any good work from teaching to forestry, writing to masonry. In reflecting on his work, Berry writes, "Works of imagination come of an impulse to transcend the limits of experience or provable knowledge in order to make a thing that is whole."[28] It is by way of imagination that we can do what no human can properly do—to see how things fit together in their past and present, the relationships of the present, and the future trajectory that the reality might take.

"What one actually or provably knows about an actual experience is never complete," writes Berry, "it cannot, within the limits of memory or factual records, be made whole. Imagination 'completes the picture' by transcending the actual memories and provable facts."[29] It is for this reason that Berry has created a kind of fictional account of his place in the Port William stories.

The fictional Port William is a different place from Berry's actual community in Port Royal, but it is dependent upon the real place, the real people, the real farms and landscapes that surround it. But to approach those directly would be to leave something out—Berry approaches them through imagination as a way to bring a wholeness that would be hard to accomplish with the limits of actual memory and understanding. Through imagination, he can tell the truth of the place in a better way than with mere memory, which in its incompleteness, might verge on a lie. So it is that a book like *Andy Catlett: Early Travels*, based on Berry's memories and experiences as a child among his relatives, is also different and more coherent than those memories.

In a way, imagination does the work that is perverted by abstraction. Abstraction in our language and thus our thinking is a means to universalize and attempt to make whole, but it fails to do so because to make whole, one must bring together many places and pieces. Abstraction obscures these and instead totalizes and incorporates all into a vague completeness. "Abstraction is the enemy *wherever* it is found," writes Berry in his essay "Out of Your Car, Off Your Horse."[30] It is abstraction, in fact, that is "the evil of the industrial economy…[with] its inability to distinguish one place or person or creature from another."[31]

The answer is a careful specificity of our language. Berry finds this exhibited in the work of E.M. Forster, a novelist to whom Berry returns regularly in his writing. In Forster, Berry finds a writer who is able to use language rooted in the particular that draws toward wholeness. As he writes of *Howard's End*:

> The great reassurance of Forster's novel is the whole-heartedness of his language. It is to begin with a language not disturbed by mystery, by things unseen. But Forster's interest throughout is in soul-sustaining habitations: houses, households, earthly places where lives can be made and loved. In defense of such dwellings he uses, without irony or apology, the vocabulary that I have depended on in this talk: truth, nature, imagination, affection, love, hope, beauty, joy. Those words are hard to keep still within definitions; they make the dictionary hum like a beehive. But in such words, in their resonance within their histories and in their associations with one another, we find our indispensable humanity, without which we are lost and in danger.[32]

This is language that recognizes its limits and by accepting them creates an opening for the transcendent. Like all good work and good economies, such language works within a scale that is proper to its place and where affection is therefore possible. "When one works beyond the reach of one's love for the place one is working in and for the things and creatures one is working with and among, then destruction inevitably results," writes Berry.[33] The answer to this is "an adequate local culture" which "keeps work within the reach of love."[34] So it is that affection, rooted in love for his particular place, has formed Berry's language and offered the standard for his work: "Hovering over nearly everything I have written is the question of how a human economy might be conducted with reverence, and therefore with due respect and kindness toward everything that is involved."[35]

It is by way of the imagination, forming and making whole his language, that Berry has come to understand his place. "By means of the imagined place," he writes, "I have learned to see my native landscape and neighborhood as a place unique in the world, a work of God, possessed of an inherent sanctity that mocks any human valuation that can be put upon it."[36]

By being subject to this subject, he has tried to tell its truth in all of its wholeness and toward its health. "If anything I have written in this place can be taken to countenance the misuse of it, or to excuse anybody for rating the land as 'capital' or its human members as 'labor' or 'resources,' my writing would have been better unwritten."[37] Such a standard is the proper standard of any language—what we say and write—that seeks to live in fidelity to the truth that will set us free.

CHAPTER ELEVEN

Peaceableness

• • • • • • • • • • • • • • • • •

LIVING IN HARMONY WITH THE WHOLE OF CREATION

After a recent terrorist attack on American soil by a sole perpetrator acting alone, a day did not pass before politicians began to speak of war. And while the United States has been at war since 2001 on several fronts in an attempt to defeat terrorism, we have not defeated terrorism, and so the only hope for peace, in the political mind, is more war.

There is some danger in focusing too much on a more recent example. But the experience of history teaches that the headlines have changed very little in the past century. In looking at Berry's work too, only the names of the wars and enemies have changed as Berry has called out the lies and pretentions of war and instead taken up the Gospel's call to "love thy enemies."

The call for peace is not a side interest or pet project for Berry; peaceableness lies at the heart of his vision for the given life. To be peaceable reflects the nature of creation and the creature within it. It responds to Jesus's call of love that extends beyond the bounds of family and tribe. This call is ultimately a call to become more fully ourselves—to become more fully human.

In his vision, Berry is not far, as we have indicated before, from the fourth-century theologian St. Augustine's understanding of peace in the creation. In working to sort out the differences between the "City of God" and the "City of Man," Augustine turned toward their founding myths. In the Genesis story of the creation of the world, which represents the founding of the "City of God," the cosmos comes to be through harmony and interconnection. Each part of it is declared good.

Rome, which represents the "City of Man" for Augustine, understood its origin to lie in the violent conflict of two brothers—Romulus and Remus. Its peace was established through violence and was thereafter made through violence. The much-lauded "Pax Romana" was achieved through war, cults of empire, and constant military occupation.

Berry follows Augustine in understanding that the creation, properly understood, is a domain whose default is peace. If we are to live our lives into our givenness, accepting our form and truth as creatures, then we must also accept this peace as our default. The achievement of any peace that comes through violence against people or the land is a false peace, a victory whose fruits are bound to be as temporary as any empire. They are the mark of a disease.

Among the first wars with which Berry engaged was the war in Vietnam. His diagnosis of the problem there is one that began the argument he's continued into his critique of the war on terror. "I am opposed to our war in Vietnam," Berry wrote in 1968, "because I see it as a symptom of a deadly illness of mankind—the illness of selfishness and pride and greed, which, empowered by modern weapons and technology, now threatens to destroy the world."[1]

This disease is one that is not distant from the disease of industrialism. The two are linked because they stem from a common view of the world.

In addressing the first Gulf War, Berry wrote, "our latest failure to be peaceable, was thus linked to a larger failure: the failure of those who most profit from the world to be able to imagine the world except in terms of abstract quantities."[2] Industrial war and industrial economies both reduce the world into simple objects, conforming to simple objectives carried out to fulfill short-term goals. In the industrial economy, a place, however long-storied, loved, and lived in, becomes known by no other measure than the money to be made on it or from it. The reduction of people and place is similar in industrial warfare.

"Modern war and modern industry are much alike, not just in their technology and methodology but in this failure of imagination," writes Berry. "There can be little doubt that industrial disfigurements of nature and industrial diminishments of human beings prepare the souls of nations for industrial war in which places become 'enemy territory,' people become 'targets' or 'collateral casualties,' and bombing sorties become 'turkey shoots.'"[3]

Industrialism helps us get into the habits of loss, sacrificing for an abstract good; it accustoms us to the routine violence of "progress." Go to any land clearing project that has wiped away a forest for a shopping center or timber, and what you will find there is destruction akin to war—eroding soil stripped bare, the twisted remains of trees pushed aside by bulldozers— there is no way to describe it but as violence. But question the necessity of this violence, and we will be told that it is the way of the world, a necessary "creative destruction" that will give us places to shop or boxes in which to receive our Amazon orders with same-day delivery. These are the habits that in Berry's mind prepare us to accept the collateral damage that comes from the "securing of our safety"; the terror we are willing to inflict to rid the world of terror.

This destructive economy reveals the failure of any measure of war as means of protection or homeland security in an age in which we have no homeland. Such measures, writes Berry, "cannot protect us against the destruction of our own land by ourselves. They cannot protect us against the selfishness, wastefulness, and greed that we have legitimized here as economic virtues, and have taught to the world."[4]

A strategy of "national security" cannot function in any legitimate way when it "cannot protect us from what may prove the greatest danger of all: the estrangement of our people from one another and from our land."[5] The loss of place, of our understanding of our lives as entangled in a membership of the whole of a place and its people, is a part of the peaceful life of the creation for which Industrial economies and war can provide no help. "Increasingly, Americans…have in this 'homeland,'" Berry writes, "no home *place* that they are strongly moved to know or love or use well or protect."[6]

Berry is helpful here in enabling us to imagine what an authentic patriotism looks like. To be a patriot, we must have a place, a land that we love. Such a love cannot be abstract; it is rooted in the particulars of the place. It is impossible then that any real patriotism could arise from industrialism. Instead, such an economy can only result in the dangerous patriotism of abstract power and symbols. As Berry writes, "War always encourages a patriotism that means not love of county but unquestioning obedience to power."[7] As such this patriotism is a subversion of the *patria*, the land from which we come, as are the wars executed in its name. "What we are doing, as we prepare for and prosecute wars allegedly for national defense," writes Berry, "is squandering in the most prodigal manner the natural and human resources of the nation."[8]

The correction to this, for Berry, is not a refusal of patriotism but an embrace of an authentic patriotism. This patriotism will not be characterized by flag waving, but by a critical engagement with anyone or any institution that might harm the homeland. "An inescapable requirement of true patriotism, love for one's land," writes Berry, "is a vigilant distrust of any determinative power, elected or unelected, that may preside over it."[9] This citizenship requires "devotion and dedication," he said; it requires us to be our best selves, calling for "all the virtues, all of one's attention, all the knowledge one can gain and bring to bear, all the powers of one's imagination and conscience and feeling."[10] It is in this love for the household in which our lives make sense that peace, which is really also health, can be possible. To imagine a politics or defense of home that threatens that health is incoherent.

True citizenship and patriotism are rooted in a proper understanding of scale and our dependencies. "My devotion thins as it widens," writes Berry. But though his care for his home *county* is greater than his care for his home *country*, he does not "care more for the United States of America than for the world."[11]

Though Berry sees such care as a challenge to the proper scale of human action, he also recognizes that "the most meaningful dependence of my house is not on the U.S. government, but on the world, the earth."[12] He means here not the abstract collection of nations and economies, but the sphere of life and the systems on which life is dependent—the cycles of sunlight and nutrients and water, the whole of the ecosystem. If we forget the poles of earth and home, then our households and "the earth must become victim of [human] institutions, the violent self-destructive machinery of man-in-the-abstract."[13] To protect ourselves from such a destruction, we must keep our allegiances in order: "To assert that a man owes an allegiance that is antecedent to his allegiance to his household, or higher than his allegiance to the earth, is to invite a state of moral chaos that will destroy both the household and the earth."[14]

* * *

Berry's vision of peace is rooted in the call of Jesus to "love your enemies" and "bless those that curse you." This call is "the greatest challenge ever laid before us, the most comprehensive vision of human progress, the best advice and the least obeyed."[15] This love for enemy is not abstract; it is radically particular because it is rooted in our encounter with our neighbors, those near to us—enemy, family, or friend. We may well be able to hate at a distance, but we cannot love at a distance. Love must entail the possibility of embrace; it must be possible to practice. "We are to love one another, and this love is to be more comprehensive than our love for family and friends and tribe and nation," Berry writes. "We are to love our neighbors though they may be strangers to us. We are to love our enemies. And this is to be a practical love; it is to be practiced, here and now."[16]

In order for this love to be practiced, we must engage our imaginations so that we can see our neighbors and enemies within their wholeness. This is the condition of charity whether personal or national. "The commandment to 'Love your enemies suggests that charity must be without limit; it must include everything. A nation's charity must come from the heart and the imagination of its people," writes Berry. "It requires us ultimately to see the world as a community of all the creatures, a community which, to be possessed by any must be shared by all."[17]

As we've noted before, imagination is the means by which we "transcend the limits of experience or provable knowledge in order to make a thing that is whole." This is necessary in all of our work and understanding, but it takes on a different kind of urgency in the work of peaceableness. If we cannot imagine our enemies, if we cannot begin to see them as bearers of God's image, then it will be easier to kill them. And so it goes for both sides of the conflict, both seeing the other only as a monster, something inhuman reduced to the act of violence and its retribution.

In order for us to be peaceable we must learn to imagine other lives. It is, Berry suggests, "imperative to imagine the lives of beings who are not ourselves and are not like ourselves: animals, plants, gods, spirits, people of other countries and other races, people of the other sex, place—and enemies."[18] Berry has done this in his fiction, imagining not only the lives of the varied people of the Port William membership, but even some of its animals from mice to turtles. It may seem a silly suggestion, that learning to imagine the lives of animals or other people could help one imagine the life of an enemy, but there is psychological evidence that bears this out. It has been shown that people who read literary fiction are more empathetic than those who don't.[19] It seems that there is something about learning to imagine someone else's life that can enable one to see how, for instance, a young man might be able to join a terrorist group.

To engage in this work of imagination, Berry says that "we must not allow public emotion or the public media to caricature our enemies."[20] For instance, if the West has conceived of Islamic nations or people as our enemies, then Berry suggests, "our schools should begin to teach the histories, cultures, arts, and languages of the Islamic nations."[21] Just as critically, he says, "our leaders should have the humility and wisdom to ask the reasons some of those people have for hating us."[22] It is through such knowledge that we can engage in the kind of imagination that allows us to see our enemies, not as "monsters" bent on some abstract vengeance, but as people who are likely engaged in the same failure of imagination as we are, people who also fail to see us as human creatures. We do not break this failure through war; the cycle can only be broken by love.

In order to engage this love we must engage in peaceableness; we must take it up as a practice. The theologian Stanley Hauerwas has often quipped that the problem with "pacifism" is that it is "so damn passive." Hauerwas, himself an advocate of peaceableness, hopes that Christians will understand that this call is not a call to do nothing, but a call to engage in the constructive and difficult disciplines of peace.

Likewise, Berry sees peaceableness as an active practice that requires more strength, intelligence, and character than any war—whatever its virtues. "Authentic peace is no more passive than war," Berry argues. "Like war, it calls for discipline and intelligence and strength of character, though it calls also for higher principles and aims. If we are serious about peace, then we must work for it as ardently, seriously, continuously, carefully, and bravely as we now prepare for war."[23]

. . .

"If [peaceableness] is not a practical and a practicable method, it is nothing," writes Berry. "As a practicable method, it reduces helplessness in the face of conflict. In the face of conflict, the peaceable person may find several solutions, the violent person only one."[24] But this practice is not one that simply responds to a conflict—it is an ongoing way of life that enables us to live into the state of peace at the center of the cosmos rather than impose our will on it through violence. It is the life by which we enter and stay close to the default of creation, a realm in which conflict and violence are aberrations, harmony and fittingness are the standard.

Like war, this practice will require sacrifice in terms of the current economy, but it is a sacrifice that aims at the enlargement of life and livelihood rather than its destruction. As Berry writes, "if we want to be at peace, we will have to waste less, spend less, use less, want less, need less."[25]

Our standards and desires, trained in the industrial economy, should conform to the ways of peace and break with the economy of violence:

> We must recognize that the standards of the industrial economy lead inevitably to war against humans just as they lead inevitably to war against nature. We must

learn to prefer quality over quantity, service over profit, neighborliness over competition, people and other creatures over machines, health over wealth, a democratic prosperity over centralized wealth and power, economic health over "economic growth."[26]

Berry's insight here is that violence and its ways are not primarily exercised in war, though they manifest themselves there in the most apparent way. Underlying the extreme of war is an everyday violence that we commit with a smile in pursuit of what might be seen as the goods of everyday comfort. Violence is not simply bombs blasting, but is more commonly the everyday life of children playing on a TruGreen yard whose nitrogen runs to the Gulf of Mexico where algae blooms to create miles of "dead-zone" in which nothing can live.

This everyday violence of the industrial economy is in the plastic toys that last only a season and tomorrow will whirl in the gyre of trash spinning in the Pacific Ocean. It is a violence that comes in the convenience of cars, the price of cheap goods and cheap labor, the subsidized deserts of corn that fuel our high fructose habits.

So it is that we must answer this violence not simply with acquiescence, but with a life that buys one thing that will last over a dozen things that won't; that purchases food that will nourish over food that leaves us and the world hungry and unhealthy. It is a way of life that will seek to make rather than buy, to accept rather than take.

This vision of peaceableness is made clear in Berry's response to the attacks of September 11, 2001. In his essay "Thoughts in the Presence of Fear," Berry lays out an alternative to the call that quickly came from President George W. Bush to go shopping. Instead of this, Berry writes that, "Starting with the economies of food and farming, we should promote at home and encourage abroad the ideal of local self-sufficiency. We should recognize that this is the surest, the safest, and the cheapest way for the world to live."[27]

This call to "go farming" might seem as simplistic a response as "go shopping" in the face of a devastating attack, but it is a response that calls us into a different rhythm and way than that of shopping. Such a response draws us into the forms of life that conform to peace—it brings us back to the earth where we can be remade.

It is the preservation of this earth with its capacities to heal that we must work to keep and restore if we hope for peace to be possible. So it is that Berry calls on us to also take up the task to "renew and extend our efforts to protect the natural foundations of the human economy: soil, water, and air." These are our life sources, and it is by remaining in harmony with them that peace can be possible. "We should protect every intact ecosystem and watershed that we have left," writes Berry, "and begin restoration of those that have been damaged."[28]

This is the long and difficult work that is before us if we desire to answer the call of peace. We will need more courage than required by any war to begin it. The results of this work, however, will be not the scars and damage of war, but the health and wholeness of beauty. "This would be work worthy of the name 'human,'" writes Berry. "It would be fascinating and lovely."[29]

CHAPTER TWELVE

· · ·

The Prophet

· · · · · · · · · · · · · · · · · · ·

LAMENT, IMAGINATION, AND THE RENEWAL OF RELIGION

Elijah in the wilderness on the run because of his challenge to the corrupt royalty; John the Baptist, on the margins of Jerusalem, a wild man calling for repentance; St. Francis, shunning wealth in favor of an economy of gifts and penance; Dorothy Day, calling for all God's people to live in the generous life that could welcome the miracle of feeding thousands; Martin Luther King, Jr., refusing the violence of his enemies and seeking liberation through love—all of these are people who took up the mantel of the prophet, even if some wouldn't have claimed it for themselves. Each mixed a call for the renewal of religion with acts of social imagination that helped unleash new possibilities in the world, God's kingdom breaking through.

Is Wendell Berry among their ranks? Is he also a prophet?

Poet, essayist, philosopher, novelist, teacher, farmer, yes, all could tag and label Wendell Berry. And as we've already said, "amateur" could be added to any of these because it marks the mode and motivation of his work—a work born and directed by love. But much of Berry's work also fits the prophetic mode, not only calling for a new way to live, but also a renewal of religion and worship—a key aspect in the traditional definition of the prophet. Berry is someone who shows us new forms of hope, but at the same time, he offers it against a background of lament. He criticizes traditional religion, but he sees roots in it that can be cultivated toward renewal.

• • •

Lament is a practice that has fallen out of favor along with confession and penance. We are told to "think positive," to greet the world with a smile, eschewing the downers that might conflict with our consumerist life. When something truly tragic happens, we do not know how to respond other than to repeat the happy patterns, to engage in the optimism that will keep everything humming along as it was. When the attacks of September 11 came, for instance, the nation was still in shock when the call came to go shopping, and soon after, we heard the magic pronouncement of war. There was no time for silence, no time to simply sit with the absurdity of violence and death. It is against such a tendency that Berry engages in prophetic lament.

His essay "Thoughts in the Presence of Fear," in response to the September 11, 2001, attacks, begins with these words: "The time will soon come when we will not be able to remember the horrors of September 11 without remembering also the unquestioning technological and economic optimism that ended on that day."[1] He goes on to cite this economy as one "founded upon the oppressive labor of poor people all around the world." The free market lauded after the attacks was one to which, Berry writes, our nation had given "the status of a religion, and were sacrificing to it their farmers, farmlands, and rural communities, their forests, wetlands, and prairies, their ecosystems and watersheds."[2]

These words are strong, painful, and biting; they are close to the prophet Jeremiah, who mourned the fall of an unrepentant people who wouldn't change their ways until there were no more ways to change. While we want to skip ahead to the hope, the prophetic vision begins by bringing us into the desert of reality. As writer Tim Suttle writes of the prophetic vocation: *"The task of the prophet is not initially to lead a movement toward social renewal, but to lead the people in creative, artistic, public lament"* (emphasis his).[3]

In Berry's essays, he begins this work of public lament, helping us to envision the brokenness of our relationships with the world, our obscured creatureliness. But it is in his poetry that Berry draws closest to the modes of the prophets of old.

Poetry has always been a primary form for prophetic lament. The Hebrew prophets often spoke in verse, and even the pronouncements of someone like Peter Maurin, cofounder of the Catholic Worker Movement, came in the form of verse, his "easy essays." Though we often ignore the fact, a great many of the biblical psalms are in fact prophetic and many take the form of lament. Hear the tones of sorrow, for instance, in these opening lines of Psalm 60:

> O God, you have rejected us, broken our defenses;
> you have been angry; now restore us!
> You have caused the land to quake; you have torn it open;
> repair the cracks in it, for it is tottering.
> You have made your people suffer hard things;
> you have given us wine to drink that made us reel.
> (60:1–3)

Berry is then in good company and a long tradition when he writes poems such as his first Sabbath poem of 1991:

The year begins with war.
Our bombs fall day and night,
Hour after hour, by death
Abroad appeasing wrath,
Folly, and greed at home.[4]

In this poem, Berry expresses the grief of war, not only in its death and violence, but in its folly. The war is not the source of lament, but the symptom of a deeper unrest—a violence rooted in the comfortable lives of normal American economic life. The poem turns biting as Berry, sounding like Jeremiah of Lamentations, proclaims:

This is a nation where
no lovely thing can last.

It is a kind of prophetic hyperbole, but it carries with it the call to wonder at its truth. What in our economy, our politics, work toward the preservation of the good? Then Berry comes down with his most troubling condemnation:

Highway and shopping mall
Still guarantee the right
And liberty to be
A peaceful murderer,
A murderous worshipper,
A slender glutton, or
A healthy whore...[5]

In this aching, sorrowful poem, Berry points to the ways in which our everyday lives are violent. It is not only by picking up guns to go and kill our enemies that we are engaged in the transgressions against the world. We have created an economy and way of life where we are violent simply by maintaining a beautiful green lawn, guaranteed by polluting chemicals, or are able to look slender, stylish, and healthy at the expense of the health of the community of creation and in fact our own ultimate well-being.

This Sabbath poem is one whose lines have stayed with me for many years, answering my own sadness at times and bringing me to it at others. Some have celebrated Berry as a writer of hope and joy, and those are certainly themes and realities in his work. But to read Berry is not always a happy thing, nor should it be. There are times after reading Berry's work that I have felt overcome by melancholy.

When one begins to see the world with Berry's eyes, it is difficult to remain comfortable, much less unchanged. Berry shows us so well how far we've drifted from our lives as creatures, living in the abundant grace of the world, that one cannot move through daily life without it becoming an invitation for lament. A trip to the grocery store becomes an exercise in despair as one begins to see, on aisle after aisle, the end products of an agricultural economy that destroys the health of land, community, and creation. A drive in a car becomes a reminder of the pollution of the petroleum economy and its speed and distance, so out of scale with human life. Berry helps tune our hearts, minds, and vision to the world so that a careful reader cannot help but see these truths all around and so cannot help but lament our condition.

Sackcloth and ashes are the garb of lament. They signify our barrenness, but they also signal the hope of our return. Lament brings us back to the soil. Like the liturgy of Ash Wednesday when Christians are reminded that "you are but dust and to dust you will return," Berry's work draws us back to the soil, where we can begin to imagine a different way toward growth and wholeness.

After we have begun to lament the systems that produce the food in our grocery stores, we can begin to work toward alternatives. Even large grocery stores now tout "local" produce, and farmers markets have never been more popular. These are changes that are borne from the work of Berry and others like Michael Pollan—writers who began by engaging us in lament for our broken food system and then turned us toward a different path which some are beginning to follow.

In his book *The Prophetic Imagination*, Walter Bruggemann writes: "*The task of prophetic ministry is to nurture, nourish, and evoke a consciousness and perception alternative to the consciousness and perception of the dominant culture around us*" (emphasis his).[6]

This is a task that begins in lament, but moves from it into a new form of social imagination and hope. And while such imagination and hope might be secular, the prophet works from a return to the ground toward a vision of the ultimate. This vision touches on the deepest parts of who we are; it delves deeply into the humming engine of our lives which is our heart, our spirit.

So it is that Berry's work as a prophet is engaged in the call to religious people to live into the truth of their faith. And while he finds much to laud and appreciate in other traditions from Taoism to Buddhism, Berry finds himself in the religion of his upbringing and forebears—Christianity, a language he finds as native as English. It is from the traditions and texts of this religion that Berry works to form the call for an alternative future to the dominant, co-opting realities of our age.

As has been evident from our previous chapters, Berry's engagement with religion is thorough: Christian understandings and scriptures, as well as the literature of Dante, Shakespeare, and Milton derived from them, permeate Berry's writings. There are two particular essays, however, that offer an essential view into Berry's role as prophet: "The Gift of Goodland" and "Christianity and the Survival of Creation."

In "The Gift of Goodland," Berry sets out with two purposes. The first is to create an argument for ecological care and responsibility rooted in the Bible. Since such responsibility must include working landscapes in addition to wild ones, Berry also necessarily includes agriculture in the scope of his argument. The second purpose is to work out the practical implications of this responsibility. If we are so called to responsibility, what does this mean in our lives? This is a question of ethics.

In these two moves, Berry is guiding us through the necessary next steps of the prophetic work. After naming our condition and calling us to lament, we must begin the work of imagination by looking to the roots of our tradition for sources of authentic reality against the lies that we've been told. Once we begin to have a grasp of this reality, then we can begin the new work of imagining and embodying the alternative kingdom it represents.

To begin these tasks, Berry takes up the account of the gift of the Promised Land to Israel rather than the more typical text for creation care, the Genesis 1—2 account. Berry finds the gift of the Promised Land a more serviceable story "because the Promised Land is a divine gift to a *fallen* people" (emphasis his).[7] It is in fact the use and abuse, the giving and taking of the Promised Land that animates much of biblical history and prophecy. It is a conditional gift that requires something of the people who would receive it. It is therefore in this story that Berry finds a tradition that might enable us to find "the definition of an ecological discipline."[8]

Central to an ecological discipline rooted in the idea of a given land is the knowledge of who gives and who receives. It is knowledge, in other words, of who is God and who is not. Berry points to the Old Testament book of Deuteronomy, where such knowledge is one of the conditions of the gift of the Promised Land: "Do not say to yourself, 'My power and the might of my own hand have gotten me this wealth.' But remember the Lord your God, for it is he who gives you power to get wealth, so that he may confirm his covenant that he swore to your ancestors, as he is doing today" (Deuteronomy 8:17–18).

This passage points to the dangers of hubris, which as Berry writes, "is the great ecological sin, just as it is the great sin of politics."[9] Hubris is the temptation to act as though we are gods and this warning against it contains the idea of propriety, the principle that "we must not use the world as though we created it ourselves."[10]

This prophetic reorientation begins to point us in a different direction. If we have realized the failure of our attempts to play god, to violate the conditions of the gift by acting as though we, in fact, "did it on our own," then we can begin to move in a different direction.

Berry finds guidance for the turn in Leviticus 25:23, in which the divine voice proclaims: "The land shall not be sold forever: for the land is mine; for ye are strangers and sojourners with me" (KJV). Here Berry finds that "what is given is not ownership, but a sort of tenancy, the right of habitation and use."[11]

We must accept the land with a carefulness and tenuousness, it is owned by someone else who could issue harsh penalties for our failure to care.

To offer a crass example, the vision Berry puts forth here is a bit like a rental vehicle verses one's own car owned outright. While I try to care for my family's car, I do not worry too much about the inevitable nicks and dings that come from parking lots or toddlers. When, however, I've been in possession of a rental car, I am extremely careful, constantly worried about something that might result in a charge. If we are responsible, we tend to treat things that we do not own with a care not given to things we own outright. This is born of the sense of propriety and also the fear of penalties, social or otherwise. We do not want to over step our bounds as mere users. So it is with the world and our use of it.

To instruct us in this use, in Berry's view, God offers us the Sabbath. When, every seven years, the land was to lie fallow, the people of God had a ritual means of realizing their limits. "Looking at their fields, the people are to be reminded that the land is theirs only by gift;" writes Berry, "it exists in its own right, and does not begin or end with any human purpose."[12] Their use of it for the other six years would then be disciplined with this knowledge.

The gift of this good land is conditional. This is a way of reminding the people that it is a grace, not something that they earned or deserve. Looking at the biblical witness, Berry discerns three means by which the people are able to preserve their place on the land, to properly accept its gift. "First of all," writes Berry, "they must be faithful, grateful, and humble."[13] The people must live themselves as creatures, rather than gods.

"Second, they must be neighborly."[14] The people must live within the bounds of their needs and make space for others. And finally, the possessors of the land must "practice good husbandry."[15] By this, Berry means that they must protect the sources of the land and their own renewal within it. The people can eat the offspring, but not the breeding stock. They can feast on the produce, but not the seed.

It is in this last point, particularly, that Berry finds "an elaborate understanding of charity." The Bible presents a vision of the land and community that recognizes that "it is a contradiction to love your neighbor and despise the great inheritance on which his life depends."[16] This brings us to the practical work of enacting this vision. As a prophet, Berry moves from opening an alternative vision of life rooted in our best traditions toward imagining the living out of that vision. So it is that he writes:

> Real charity calls for the study of agriculture, soil husbandry, engineering, architecture, mining, manufacturing, transportation, the making of monuments and pictures, songs and stories. It calls not just for skills but for the study and criticism of skills, because in all of them a choice must be made: they can be used either charitably or uncharitably.[17]

To love, we must be able to enact love, and we must be able to do it day in and day out in our work. It is this love that will guide us away from the carelessness that leads us to the destruction of the world and our neighbors through our everyday, middle-class existence of buying plastics, fertilizing lawns, eating cheap food, and driving to soccer practices. It is love that will ultimately move us toward being good and therefore doing good.

"In order to be good, you have to know how," writes Berry, "and this knowing is vast, complex, humble and humbling; it is of the mind and of the hands, of neither alone."[18] It is knowledge that requires a spirit and a body and so brings us necessarily to the question of livelihood.

Within Buddhism, there is a principle called "right-livelihood." It is a call for work to be good, not only in its execution, but in its alignment with goodness. Since Buddhists are to be peaceable, then it would be a violation of this principle for a Buddhist to make a living from the manufacture and sale of weapons, for example. Berry finds in the biblical reorientation of our vision the very practical question of in what kind of livelihood which we might rightly engage. "If 'the earth is the Lord's' and we are His stewards, then obviously some livelihoods are 'right' and some are not," writes Berry.[19]

This is a critical and haunting question. It requires reflection and it requires a community in which the answers to such questions can be had.

Early in my working life, I was employed by a company that served the needs and interests of many large corporations. I struggled with the job, especially as I read Berry's work, but at the time, none of the companies we served were inherently harmful to the world. In time, however, the company began to engage some clients whose businesses were built on the kinds of destruction of which Berry is speaking. I decided that it was time for me to leave the company.

I was fortunate in that I was able to find other work fairly quickly, but it may not be so easy for others. This is why to live into the prophet's call we must have a community that can enable us to hear it and answer the hard truths of the message.

What if, for instance, churches were there to tell members in such difficult situations that they will be taken care of until they find other work? It is a bold vision, but one that does exist in some places. I have known of churches that have helped their members find livelihoods that were right, leave those that weren't, and be able to survive financially in the meantime.

More of such church communities would likely exist if only more people were willing to take the risks that require them. It is the voice of the prophet that helps call us to take just that kind of chance. It is a call to risk righteousness against idolatry.

• • •

Berry's essay "Christianity and the Survival of Creation" is a text that challenges Christianity to accept the radical truths of its scriptures, and this too is a common thread of the prophetic tradition. Berry critiques and addresses Christian institutions head-on, not as an outsider but in the name of their deeper truths.

Taking up the clearly bad examples of the faithful's failure to care for the creation, Berry suggests that if we were only to read the Bible, we would discover a very different vision. Such discoveries include the realities that the earth is the Lord's, that we are members of creation not its masters, that the world is called "good" by God and was made for his pleasure. The biblical picture, Berry concludes, is that "we are holy creatures living among other holy creatures in a world that is holy."[20] If this is our biblical inheritance, then how has Christianity moved so far from these truths in both belief and practice?

The answer is, in part, that Christians have separated religion and economy. For Berry, the most urgent question before Christians is this: "What sort of economy would be responsible to the holiness of life?"[21] It is a question for which Berry believes no "organized Christianity now has any idea."[22] But Christianity must get an idea, because to fail to have one is to fail to live into the faith's true call. Christianity itself is at risk if it cannot answer this question of economy.

The other trouble that institutional Christianity brings to this task of caring for the creation is its overly narrow view of holy places, particularly as contained and embodied in church buildings. "The idea of the exclusive holiness of church buildings is, of course, wildly incompatible with the idea, which the churches also teach, that God is present in all places to hear prayers," writes Berry.[23] In this statement he is very close to a long prophetic tradition that has challenged holy places and religious acts that presume to contain or manipulate God.[24]

Having become so enclosed and separated from the holy life of the everyday, Berry writes that "modern Christianity has become willy-nilly the religion of the state and the economic status quo."[25] It has become an ally of what should be its enemy, the companion and aid to the Caesars of our age. "It has admired Caesar and comforted him in his depredations and defaults," writes Berry. "But in its de facto alliance with Caesar, Christianity connives directly in the murder of creation."[26] These are strong words, but such is the bite of a prophet's voice. It is a call not simply of condemnation, but rather a mirror to show us what we've become—a truth that can transform.

Rather than ignore Berry's challenge, we should bring it back to our churches, look hard at one another, and begin to go outside, searching for the soil from which we might be renewed. It is work that is happening all around the country as churches and religious communities are beginning to accept the prophet's call and imagine a different way. Let me close then with one example that would, I think, earn Berry's smile.

On a highway on the eastern edge of Naples, Florida, Cornerstone United Methodist Church sits on a campus of several acres. With land to spare, they began a modest project of gardening. Members of the community joined them and with time the land around the church became more than a garden, it is to any eye, practically a farm, a working orchard and vegetable garden. It uses organic methods, mixing perennials and annuals in a pattern that works from nature's example.

But more than this, the church has begun to pay attention to where it is, where its water flows and what ecosystem it belongs to. They discovered that they are a part of the Corkscrew Swamp Watershed, a historic, ecologically important watershed that hosts an Audubon bird sanctuary. The church now owns this reality and connects with the swamp in numerous ways, even taking their youth groups on regular trips to visit the sanctuary.

Through these activities and many others, the church is becoming placed and present to its place. It is becoming harder for its members, when asked where they worship, to point to the buildings. They are learning, through imaginations prophetically engaged, that the holy is everywhere and that their responses of worship should be as well. When the prophet calls, there are always some who will answer.

AFTERWORD

A CONVERSATION WITH WENDELL BERRY

As I wrote this book, there were many questions that came as I reflected on Berry's work. Some were answered in continued reading, but others still lingered. With paper and a postal stamp, using his preferred mode of communication, I sent Berry six questions whose answers I thought would be helpful for readers to move from reading into the practice of creatureliness. Berry was kind enough to respond with his signature combination of economy and wisdom.

The idea that our lives are "given" comes up often in your writing. What does it mean to be given? How does it change how we live in the world?

I use the word "given" in reference to this world and our life in it. Two things are implied: first, that we ourselves did not make these things, although by birth we are made responsible for them; and, second, that the world and our lives in it do not come to us by chance.

St. Bernard of Clairvaux once wrote: "The way is humility, the goal is truth." Your own work reflects a similar understanding. How does humility help us recover the truth about the world and ourselves?

If you think, as I do, that the truth is large and our intelligence small, then a certain humility is implied and is even inescapable. As for my own humility, I am not very certain about the extent of it. I know that I had my upbringing from people who would have been ashamed of me if they heard me bragging on myself like a presidential candidate, and I am still in agreement with them. However, I seem to have a good deal of confidence in the rightness of my advocacy for good care of the land and the people. Without that confidence, I don't think I could have kept it up for as long as I have.

For us to be healthy, we must be members of a whole, but the other side is that we are entangled in the diseases of the membership, whether we like it or not. For instance, many of us would like to be rid of fossil fuels, but cannot live lovingly in our communities without them. How do we work toward health without getting overwhelmed by these maladies common to the membership?

Advocates for good care of the land and the people are, as you say, involved inescapably in the wrongs that they oppose. I don't have a method for dealing with this. I can only try to meet my obligations the best I can with the available means. I try to keep the standard of good health always in mind. I try not to buy things I don't need. And I continue to try to support myself as much as possible by my own work. And yet I remain involved in wrongs that I recognize as such and oppose. Like everybody I know or have heard of. I call this Original Sin Round Two.

So much of your work is about place and home. Many of us who did not grow up deeply rooted in a place read your work with a sense of envy and loss. How can we begin to become a part of a place without our settling down simply being another act of choice in a consumer economy? What advice would you give someone who grew up in five different places and is now ready to "stop somewhere"?

It is true that my family on both sides has belonged to this neighborhood for a long time, and there has never been a time in my life when I did not think of it as my home. As a writer, my obligation has been to bear witness to this circumstance, which I have certainly found rewarding but not entirely so. Tanya and I, however, have not been immune to the "mobility" of our time. We have lived here now for more than fifty years. But in her young life, Tanya attended twenty-two schools. And before we finally settled here, she and I set up housekeeping more or less in ten houses. I believe we both find good reasons to be glad we have lived here so long and in my writing I probably have said enough about such reasons as we have found. But my obligation to bear witness to my own experience does not imply an obligation to advise others. It was Gary Snyder who advised that people in our generally homeless society should "stop somewhere." He very properly did not say where anybody should stop, or, once there, how to stay stopped.

For someone reading your work, daydreaming of country life while on his lunch break in downtown Chicago, what would be the first advice you would offer for him to reclaim his life as a creature?

I'm perfectly willing to recommend that people should try to understand their present circumstances and their personal economies, even that they should measure their circumstances and conduct by the standard of good health. But it is impossible to be entirely confident in advising even people you know well about their personal choices. I assume that there are some people in downtown Chicago who ought to stay in downtown Chicago.

Finally, as someone who has worked for many decades against the grain of an economy bent on destruction, what sustains you and continues to give you hope?

I am sustained by what I know of the history and present examples of good work, and by the goodness and beauty that I still find in the world.

SOURCES

· · ·

Berry, Wendell. "A Citizen's Response to the National Security Strategy," *Orion Magazine,* accessed October 18, 2016, https://orionmagazine.org/article/a-citizens-response-to-the-national-security-strategy/.

_____. *Citizenship Papers.* Washington, DC: Shoemaker & Hoard, 2003.

_____. "Faustian Economics" *Harper's Magazine.* (May, 2008): 35–42.

_____. *Hannah Coulter.* Washington, DC: Shoemaker & Hoard, 2004.

_____. *Home Economics: Fourteen Essays.* San Francisco: North Point, 1987.

_____. *Imagination in Place.* Berkeley, CA: Counterpoint, 2010.

_____. *It All Turns on Affection: The Jefferson Lecture and Other Essays.* Berkeley, CA: Counterpoint, 2012.

_____. *Jayber Crow.* Washington, DC: Counterpoint, 2000.

_____. *Leavings: Poems.* Berkeley, CA: Counterpoint, 2010.

_____. *Life Is a Miracle: An Essay Against Modern Superstition.* Washington, DC: Counterpoint, 2000.

_____. *The Long-Legged House.* New York: Harcourt, Brace, Jovanovich, 1969.

_____. *New Collected Poems.* Berkeley, CA: Counterpoint, 2012.

_____. *Our Only World: Ten Essays.* Berkeley, CA: Counterpoint, 2015.

_____. *The Art of the Commonplace: The Agrarian Essays of Wendell Berry.* Edited by Norman Wirzba. Washington, DC: Counterpoint, 2002.

_____. *The Gift of Good Land: Further Essays Cultural and Agricultural.* San Francisco: North Point, 1981.

_____. *That Distant Land: The Collected Stories.* Washington, DC: Shoemaker & Hoard, 2004.

_____. "Thoughts in the Presence of Fear," *Orion Magazine*, https://orionmagazine.org/ article/ thoughts-in-the-presence-of-fear/.

_____. *A Timbered Choir: The Sabbath Poems 1979–1997.* New York: Counterpoint, 1998.

_____. *A Turn of the Crank: Essays.* Berkeley, CA: Counterpoint, 1995.

_____. *This Day: Collected & New Sabbath Poems 1979–2013.* Berkeley, CA: Counterpoint, 2013.

_____. *The Unforeseen Wilderness: Kentucky's Red River Gorge.* Photographs by Ralph Eugene Meatyard. revised ed. Washington: Shoemaker & Hoard, 2006.

_____. *The Unsettling of America: Culture and Agriculture.* San Francisco: Sierra Club, 1977.

_____. *The Way of Ignorance and Other Essays.* Washington, DC: Shoemaker & Hoard, 2005.

_____. *What Are People For?* New York: North Point, 1990.

_____. *What Matters?: Economics for a Renewed Commonwealth,* foreword by Herman Daly. Washington, DC: Counterpoint, 2010.

CHAPTER ONE

1. "Industrial" and "Industrialism" are often capitalized in Berry's work because those terms represent an ideology and so follow the conventions for terms such as Capitalism or Communism.

2. Rowan Williams, *On Christian Theology* (Oxford: Blackwell, 2000), 77.

3. Williams, 78.

4. Williams, 77.

5. Alisdair MacIntyre, *After Virtue: A Study in Moral Theory*, second ed. (Notre Dame, IN: Notre Dame UP, 1984), 263.

6. MacIntyre, 263.

7. Gene Logsdon, *Living at Nature's Pace: Farming and the American Dream* (White River Junction, VT: Chelsea Green, 2000), xii.

8. Wendell Berry, *Blessed Are the Peacemakers: Christ's Teachings About Love, Compassion, and Forgiveness* (Washington, DC: Shoemaker & Hoard, 2005).

9. http://www.nytimes.com/2016/03/13/books/review/wendell-berry-by-the-book.html.

10. Wendell Berry, "Landsman: Jim Leach in Conversation with Wendell Berry and Tanya Berry," *It All Turns on Affection* (Berkeley, CA: Counterpoint, 2012), 44.

11. Wendell Berry, *The Unsettling of America: Culture & Agriculture* (San Francisco: Sierra Club, 1977), 17.

12. Wendell Berry, *Life Is a Miracle: An Essay Against Modern Superstition* (Washington, DC: Counterpoint, 2000), 4.

13. William Shakespeare, *King Lear*, ed. Andrew Hadfield (New York: Barnes & Noble, 2007), 4.5.48.

14. *King Lear*, IV.5.55.
15. Berry, *Life Is a Miracle*, 5.
16. Berry, *Life Is a Miracle*, 10.
17. Wendell Berry, *Citizenship Papers* (Washington, DC: Shoemaker & Hoard, 2003), 184.
18. Berry, *Citizenship Papers*, 184.
19. Wendell Berry, *This Day: Collected & New Sabbath Poems 1979–2013* (Berkeley, CA: Counterpoint, 2013), 150.

CHAPTER TWO

1. Wendell Berry, "The Way of Ignorance," *The Way of Ignorance and Other Essays* (Washington, DC: Shoemaker & Hoard, 2005), 53.
2. Berry, *The Way of Ignorance*, 63.
3. Michael Casey, *A Guide to Living in the Truth: Saint Benedict's Teaching on Humility* (Liguori, MO: Triumph, 2001), 18–19.
4. Bernard of Clairvaux, *The Steps of Humility and Pride* (Kalamazoo, MI: Cistercian, 1989), 29.
5. Berry, *Life Is a Miracle*, 11.
6. Berry, *It All Turns on Affection*, 27.
7. Berry, *Life Is a Miracle*, 13.
8. Berry, *Life Is a Miracle*, 13.
9. Berry, *Life Is a Miracle*, 13.
10. Berry, *Life Is a Miracle*, 14.
11. Berry, *It All Turns on Affection*, 25.
12. Alan Neuhauser, "BP Oil Spill Behind Die-Off of Baby Dolphins," *U.S. News & World Report*, April 12, 2016, http://www.usnews.com/news/blogs/data-mine/articles/2016-04-12/bp-deepwater-horizon-oil-spill-behind-die-off-of-baby-dolphins.
13. Berry, *What Are People For?*, 5.
14. Berry, *What Are People For?*, 5.
15. Berry, *What Are People For?*, 8.

16. Berry, *What Are People For?*, 8.
17. Berry, *What Are People For?*, 9.
18. Berry, *What Are People For?*, 9.
19. Berry, *What Are People For?*, 11.
20. Wendell Berry, *New Collected Poems*, 79.
21. Berry, *What Are People For?*, 12.
22. Ewen Callaway, "'Minimal' cell raises stakes in race to harness synthetic life," *Nature*, http://www.nature.com/news/minimal-cell-raises-stakes-in-race-to-harness-synthetic-life-1.19633.
23. Berry, *The Way of Ignorance*, 62.
24. Berry, *The Way of Ignorance*, 62.
25. Wendell Berry, "Faustian Economics," *Harpers*, May 2008: 41.
26. Wendell Berry, *Leavings: Poems* (Berkeley, CA: Counterpoint, 2010), 23.

Chapter Three

1. Wendell Berry, *New Collected Poems* (Berkeley, CA: Counterpoint, 2012), 345.
2. Charles D'Ambrosio, *Loitering: New & Collected Essays* (Portland, OR: Tin House, 2014), 73.
3. Wendell Berry, *The Art of the Commonplace: The Agrarian Essays of Wendell Berry*, ed. Norman Wirzba (Washington, DC: Counterpoint, 2002), 125.
4. Berry, *What Are People For?*, 200.
5. David Cayley, *Rivers North of the Future: The Testament of Ivan Illich* (Toronto: House of Anansi, 2005), 58.
6. Cayley, *Rivers North of the Future*, xiii.
7. Berry, *What Are People For?*, 200.
8. Simone Weil, *Waiting for God*. Trans. Emma Craufurd (New York: Perennial Classics, 2001), 89.
9. Quoted in Shane Claiborne, et. al., *Common Prayer: A Liturgy for Ordinary Radicals* (Grand Rapids: Zondervan, 2010), 275.

10. Berry, *What Are People For?*, 201.
11. Berry, *What Matters?*, 96.
12. Berry, *What Matters?*, 99.
13. Berry, *What Matters?*, 98.
14. Wendell Berry, *It All Turns on Affection: The Jefferson Lecture and Other Essay*, (Berkeley, CA: Counterpoint, 2012), 32–33.
15. Wendell Berry, *Standing By Words* (Berkeley, CA: Counterpoint, 2011), 61.
16. Wendell Berry, *Hannah Coulter* (Washington, DC: Shoemaker & Hoard, 2004), 61.
17. Wendell Berry, *Sex, Economy, Freedom, and Community: Eight Essays* (New York: Pantheon, 1993), 133.
18. Berry, *Sex, Economy, Freedom, and Community*, 137.
19. Berry, *Sex, Economy, Freedom, and Community*, 138.
20. Berry, *Sex, Economy, Freedom, and Community*, 138.
21. Wendell Berry, *That Distant Land: The Collected Stories* (Washington, DC: Shoemaker, 2004), 376.
22. Berry, *That Distant Land*, 376.
23. Berry, *That Distant Land*, 381.
24. Berry, *That Distant Land*, 381.
25. Berry, *That Distant Land*, 399.
26. Berry, *Sex, Economy, Freedom, and Community*, 139.
27. Berry, *New Collected Poems*, 168.

CHAPTER FOUR

1. Berry, "Two Economies," *Home Economics: Fourteen Essays* (San Francisco: North Point, 1987), 55.
2. Berry, *It All Turns on Affection*, 20.
3. Berry, *It All Turns on Affection*, 20.
4. Berry, *What Matters?*, 178.
5. From an energy perspective "Industrial" and "post-Industrial" are the same. Both run on the burning of fossil fuels whether one is writing software or forging steel.

6. Wendell Berry, "The Agrarian Standard," in *The Essential Agrarian Reader*, ed. Norman Wirzba (Berkeley, CA: Counterpoint, 2004), 24.
7. Berry, *Home Economics*, 70.
8. Dietrich Von Hildebrand, *Humility: Wellspring of Virtue* (Manchester, NH: Sophia, 1997), 10.
9. Berry, *Home Economics*, 68.
10. Berry, *What Matters?*, 159.
11. Berry, *What Matters?*, 159.
12. Berry, *What Matters?*, 178.
13. Berry, *What Matters?*, 179.
14. Berry, *What Matters?*, 179.
15. Berry, *Citizenship Papers*, 116.
16. Berry, "The Agrarian Standard," 24.
17. Berry, *Citizenship Papers*, 117.
18. Berry, "The Agrarian Standard," 27.
19. Berry, "The Agrarian Standard," 26.
20. Berry, "The Agrarian Standard," 30.
21. Quoted in Berry, *Citizenship Papers*, 147.
22. Berry, "The Agrarian Standard," 29.
23. Berry, *It All Turns on Affection*, 37.
24. Berry, *What Matters?*, 191.
25. Berry, *This Day*, 160.

CHAPTER FIVE
1. Berry, *What Matters?*, 189.
2. Berry, *Our Only World: Ten Essays* (Berkeley, CA: Counterpoint, 2015), 149.
3. Berry, *Our Only World*, 149.
4. Berry, *Hannah Coulter*, 133–34.
5. Berry, *The Art of the Commonplace*, 283.
6. Berry, *The Gift of Good Land: Further Essays Cultural and Agricultural* (San Francisco: North Point, 1981), 174.
7. Berry, *The Art of the Commonplace*, 290.

8. Berry, *The Art of the Commonplace*, 291.
9. Berry, *The Art of the Commonplace*, 291.
10. Berry, *What Are People For?*, 10.
11. Berry, *What Are People For?*, 170.
12. Berry, *What Are People For?*, 170.
13. Berry, *Life is a Miracle*, 21.
14. Berry, *What Are People For?*, 180.
15. Berry, *What Are People For?*, 180.
16. Berry, *What Are People For?*, 184.
17. Berry, *What Are People For?*, 181.
18. Berry, *What Are People For?*, 182.
19. Berry, *What Are People For?*, 185.
20. Berry, *What Are People For?*, 152.
21. Berry, *A Timbered Choir: The Sabbath Poems 1979–1997* (New York: Counterpoint, 1998), 167.

CHAPTER SIX

1. Wendell Berry, Foreword, in Norman Wirzba, *Living the Sabbath: Discovering the Rhythms of Rest and Delight* (Grand Rapids: Brazos, 2006), 12.
2. Berry, Foreword, *Living the Sabbath*, 12.
3. Berry, *This Day*, xxi.
4. Berry, *This Day*, xxi.
5. Berry, *This Day*, 53.
6. Berry, *This Day*, xxii.
7. Berry, *This Day*, xxii.
8. Berry, *This Day*, xxii.
9. Berry, *This Day*, xxii.
10. Wirzba, *Living the Sabbath*, 33.
11. Abraham Joshua Heschel, *The Sabbath: Its Meaning for Modern Man* (New York: Farrar, Straus, and Giroux, 2005).
12. "Berry, *This Day*, 29.
13. Berry, Foreword, *Living the Sabbath*, 11.
14. Berry, *This Day*, 181.
15. Berry, *The Unsettling of America*, 131.

16. Berry, *This Day*, xxiii.
17. Walter Brueggemann, *Sabbath as Resistance: Saying No to the Culture of Now* (Louisville, KY: Westminster John Knox, 2014), 6.
18. Berry, *This Day*, 301.
19. Brueggemann, *Sabbath as Resistance*, 45.
20. "The Ten Principles," Sabbath Manifesto, http://www. sabbathmanifesto.org/the-ten-principles/.

CHAPTER SEVEN

1. Wallace Stegner, *Angle of Repose* (New York: Penguin, 1971), 277.
2. Quoted in Jonathan Wilson-Hartgrove, *The Wisdom of Stability: Rooting Faith in a Mobile Culture* (Brewster, MA: Paraclete, 2010), 114.
3. Berry, *The Unsettling of America*, 3.
4. Berry, *The Unsettling of America*, 5.
5. Berry, *The Unsettling of America*, 7.
6. Berry, "Thoughts on Citizenship and Conscience," *The Long-Legged House* (New York: Harcourt, Brace, Jovanovich, 1969), 87.
7. Berry, *The Unsettling of America*, 9.
8. Berry, *The Unforeseen Wilderness: Kentucky's Red River Gorge*. Photographs by Ralph Eugene Meatyard. revised ed. (Washington, DC: Shoemaker & Hoard, 2006), 43.
9. Berry, "Faustian Economics," 36.
10. Wilson-Hartgrove, *The Wisdom of Stability*, 5.
11. Berry, *It All Turns on Affection*, 25.
12. Quoted in Berry, *Life Is a Miracle*, 138
13. Berry, *Life Is a Miracle*, 138
14. Naomi Klein, *This Changes Everything: Capitalism vs. The Climate* (New York: Simon & Schuster, 2015), 342.
15. Berry, *Citizenship Papers*, 34.
16. Berry, *Imagination in Place* (Berkeley, CA: Counterpoint, 2010), 11.

17. Wendell Berry, "Where Have All the Joiners Gone," *Orion Magazine*, https://orionmagazine.org/article/where-have-all-the-joiners-gone/
18. Berry, *Imagination in Place*, 10.

CHAPTER EIGHT

1. Berry, *Our Only World: Ten Essays*, 58.
2. Berry, *Our Only World*, 96.
3. Berry, *Another Turn of the Crank*, 87.
4. Berry, *Another Turn of the Crank*, 89.
5. Berry, *Another Turn of the Crank*, 101.
6. Berry, *Another Turn of the Crank*, 102.
7. Berry, *Another Turn of the Crank*, 104.
8. Berry, *That Distant Land*, 83.
9. Berry, *That Distant Land*, 121.
10. Berry, *Remembering: A Novel* (Berkeley, CA: Counterpoint, 2008), 5.
11. Berry, *Remembering*, 51.
12. Berry, *Remembering*, 121.
13. Berry, *Remembering*, 122.
14. Berry, *Remembering*, 123.
15. Berry, *Remembering*, 123.
16. Berry, *Remembering*, 123.
17. Berry, *What Are People For?*, 10.
18. Berry, *What are People For?*, 11.
19. Berry, *It All Turns on Affection*, 23.
20. Berry, *It All Turns on Affection*, 23.
21. Berry, *It All Turns on Affection*, 23.
22. Berry, *What Are People For?*, 154.
23. Berry, *What Are People For?*, 155.

CHAPTER NINE

1. Quoted in Berry, *Life Is a Miracle*, 46.
2. Berry, *Life Is a Miracle*, 54.
3. Berry, *Our Only World*, 7.

4. Berry, *The Unsetting of American*, 105.
5. Berry, *The Unsetting of American*, 108.
6. Berry, *Another Turn of the Crank*, 96.
7. Berry, *The Unsetting of American*, 103–104.
8. For a discussion of this see Rob Dunn's *The Wild Life of Our Bodies: Predators, Parasites, and Partners That Shape Who We Are Today* (New York: Harper, 2011).
9. Berry, *Art of the Commonplace*, 101.
10. Berry, *Art of the Commonplace*, 104.
11. Pope Francis, *Laudato Si'*, 155.
12. Berry, *Art of the Commonplace*, 148.
13. Berry, *Another Turn of the Crank*, 90.
14. Berry, *Art of the Commonplace*, 104.
15. Berry, *Art of the Commonplace*, 93.
16. Berry, *Art of the Commonplace*, 99–100.
17. Berry, *The Way of Ignorance*, 136.
18. Berry, *Art of the Commonplace*, 93.
19. Berry, *Art of the Commonplace*, 132–133.
20. Berry, *Art of the Commonplace*, 133.
21. Berry, *Art of the Commonplace*, 134.
22. Berry, *What Are People For?*, 140.
23. Berry, *The Unsetting of American*, 103.
24. Berry, *New Collected Poems*, 327.

CHAPTER TEN

1. Berry, *New Collected Poems*, 359.
2. Stanley Hauerwas, *Performing the Faith: Bonhoeffer and the Practice of Nonviolence* (Grand Rapids, MI: Brazos, 2004), 57.
3. Hauerwas, *Performing the Faith*, 70.
4. Berry, *Standing By Words: Essays* (Berkeley, CA: Counterpoint, 2011), 31.
5. Berry, *Standing By Words*, 29.
6. Berry, *Standing By Words*, 31.

7. Berry, *New Collected Poems*, 248.
8. Berry, *Standing By Words*, 30.
9. Berry, *Standing By Words*, 33.
10. Berry, *Standing By Words*, 33.
11. Berry, *Standing By Words*, 39.
12. Berry, *Standing By Words*, 42.
13. Berry, *Standing By Words*, 42.
14. Berry, *Standing By Words*, 47.
15. Berry, *Standing By Words*, 49.
16. Quoted in Hauerwas, *Performing the Faith*, 57.
17. Wendell Berry, "How to Be a Poet," Poetry Foundation, http://www.poetryfoundation.org/poetrymagazine/poems/detail/41087.
18. Berry, *Standing By Words*, 50.
19. Berry, *Standing By Words*, 51.
20. Berry, *Standing By Words*, 51.
21. Berry, *What Are People For?*, 65.
22. Berry, *What Are People For?*, 66.
23. Berry, *What Are People For?* 66.
24. Berry, *What Are People For?*, 67.
25. Berry, *What Are People For?*, 70.
26. Berry, *What Are People For?*, 70.
27. Berry, *What Are People For?*, 70.
28. Berry, *Imagination in Place*, 3.
29. Berry, *Imagination in Place*, 4.
30. Berry, *Sex, Economy, Freedom, & Community*, 23.
31. Berry, *Sex, Economy, Freedom, & Community*, 23.
32. Berry, "It All Turns on Affection," http://www.neh.gov/about/awards/jefferson-lecture/wendell-e-berry-lecture.
33. Berry, *Sex, Economy, Freedom, and Community*, 24.
34. Berry, "It All Turns on Affection."
35. Berry, *Imagination in Place*, 15.
36. Berry, *Imagination in Place*, 15.
37. Berry, *Imagination in Place*, 15–16.

CHAPTER ELEVEN

1. Berry, *The Long-Legged House*, 68.
2. Berry, *Sex, Economy, Freedom & Community*, 82.
3. Berry, *Sex, Economy, Freedom & Community*, 82.
4. Berry, *Citizenship Papers*, 6.
5. Berry, *Citizenship Papers*, 6.
6. Berry, *Citizenship Papers*, 6.
7. Berry, *Sex, Economy, Freedom & Community*, 76–77.
8. Berry, *Citizenship Papers*, 28.
9. Berry, "A Citizen's Response."
10. Berry, *The Long-Legged House*, 78.
11. Berry, *The Long-Legged House*, 79.
12. Berry, *The Long-Legged House*, 79.
13. Berry, *The Long-Legged House*, 79.
14. Berry, *The Long-Legged House*, 79.
15. Berry, *Citizenship Papers*, 30.
16. Berry, *The Way of Ignorance*, 134.
17. Berry, *Citizenship Papers*, 9.
18. Berry, *Economy, Freedom & Community*, 82–83.
19. Julianne Chaiet, "Novel Finding: Reading Literary Fiction Improves Empathy," *Scientific American*, http://www.scientificamerican.com/article/novel-finding-reading-literary-fiction-improves-empathy/.
20. Berry, "Thoughts in the Presence of Fear."
21. Berry, "Thoughts in the Presence of Fear."
22. Berry, "Thoughts in the Presence of Fear."
23. Berry, "A Citizen's Response."
24. Berry, *Sex, Economy, Freedom & Community*, 87.
25. Berry, *Sex, Economy, Freedom & Community*, 92.
26. Berry, *Sex, Economy, Freedom & Community*, 91.
27. Berry, "Thoughts in the Presence of Fear."
28. Berry, "Thoughts in the Presence of Fear."
29. Berry, *Our Only World*, 19.

CHAPTER TWELVE

1. Berry, "Thoughts in the Presence of Fear."
2. Berry, "Thoughts in the Presence of Fear."
3. Tim Suttle, "Prophetic Imagination by Walter Brueggemann," http://www.patheos.com/blogs/paperbacktheology/2007/10/ prophetic-imagination-by-walter-brueggemann.html.
4. Berry, *A Timbered Choir*, 125.
5. Berry, *A Timbered Choir*, 125.
6. Walter Brueggemann, *The Prophetic Imagination* (Philadelphia: Fortress, 1978). 13.
7. Berry, *The Gift of Good Land*, 169.
8. Berry, *The Gift of Good Land*, 269.
9. Berry, *The Gift of Good Land*, 270.
10. Berry, *The Gift of Good Land*, 270.
11. Berry, *The Gift of Good Land*, 271.
12. Berry, *The Gift of Good Land*, 271.
13. Berry, *The Gift of Good Land*, 272.
14. Berry, *The Gift of Good Land*, 272.
15. Berry, *The Gift of Good Land*, 272.
16. Berry, *The Gift of Good Land*, 273.
17. Berry, *The Gift of Good Land*, 274.
18. Berry, *The Gift of Good Land*, 275.
19. Berry, *The Gift of Good Land*, 275.
20. Berry, *Sex, Economy, Freedom & Community*, 99.
21. Berry, *Sex, Economy, Freedom & Community*, 100.
22. Berry, *Sex, Economy, Freedom & Community*, 100.
23. Berry, *Sex, Economy, Freedom & Community*, 100.
24. For example, Psalm 51:16, Hosea 6:6, Isaiah 1:11, and Acts 17:24.
25. Berry, *Sex, Economy, Freedom & Community*, 114.
26. Berry, *Sex, Economy, Freedom & Community*, 115.

A C K N O W L E D G M E N T S

Gratitude is a key practice in any given life and so I must express my gratitude to a few of the people who helped make this book a reality. Thank you to Jon Sweeney for first initiating the project and to my agent Wendy Sherman for helping turn an idea into a possibility. Thanks are especially due to Mark Lombard, Katie Carroll, and Ericka McIntyre at Franciscan Media for editing and shepherding the book to its completion. I am also deeply appreciative of my conversation partners Brent Laytham and Tim Sedgwick who carefully read and commented on early versions of several chapters. Finally, thank you to Emily Sutterfield, whose conversations helped bring the challenges of Berry's work into our life together.

About the Author

Ragan Sutterfield (M.Div., Virginia Theological Seminary) is ordained in the Episcopal Church and serves a parish in his native Arkansas. His writing has appeared in a variety of magazines, including: *The Christian Century, Sojourners, The Oxford American, Christianity Today,* and *Books & Culture.* He contributes regularly to the *Englewood Review of Books.*

Ragan is the author of *This Is My Body: From Obesity to Ironman, My Journey into the True Meaning of Flesh, Spirit and Deeper Faith* (Convergent/Random House 2015), *Cultivating Reality: How the Soil Might Save Us* (Cascade 2013), and the small collection of essays, *Farming as a Spiritual Discipline* based on his experiences as a one-time livestock farmer.

Ragan works to live the good and given life in partnership with his wife, Emily, and daughters, Lillian and Lucia.